Active Directory with PowerShell

Learn to configure and manage Active Directory using PowerShell in an efficient and smart way

Uma Yellapragada

BIRMINGHAM - MUMBAI

Active Directory with PowerShell

First published: January 2015

Production reference: 1200115

Published by Packt Publishing Ltd.
Livery Place
35 Livery Street
Birmingham B3 2PB, UK.

ISBN 978-1-78217-599-5

www.packtpub.com

Credits

Author

Uma Yellapragada

Reviewers

David Green

Ross Stone

Nisarg Vora

Commissioning Editor

Taron Pereira

Acquisition Editor

Sonali Vernekar

Content Development Editor

Prachi Bisht

Technical Editor

Saurabh Malhotra

Copy Editors

Heeral Bhatt

Pranjali Chury

Gladson Monteiro

Adithi Shetty

Project Coordinator

Sageer Parkar

Proofreaders

Simran Bhogal

Stephen Copestake

Martin Diver

Ameesha Green

Paul Hindle

Indexer

Hemangini Bari

Production Coordinator

Aparna Bhagat

Cover Work

Aparna Bhagat

About the Author

Uma Yellapragada has over 11 years of experience in the IT industry. Her core experience includes management of Active Directory, Microsoft Exchange, System Center Operations Manager (SCOM), Microsoft Office Communications Server (OCS/Lync), Microsoft Digital/Information Rights Management Services (DRMS/IRM), Hyper-V, VMware, PowerShell, and VBScript.

She also has experience working with process technologies such as ITIL, Six Sigma, and PMP.

She is the kind of person who challenges herself on a day-to-day basis and searches for areas of improvement as part of her work. As a result of this, she developed a passion for scripting with VBScript and PowerShell.

She blogs her activities and research at `http://techyyblog.com` and writes occasionally at `http://techibee.com`.

About the Reviewers

David Green is an IT professional from the south of England with a wealth of experience from both the public and private sectors. Currently working in the private sector for a leading food manufacturing company, David is always looking to provide robust and scalable solutions that contribute to business objectives. He writes on his blog about little projects and solutions he finds, helps where he can, and generally tries to learn something useful every day. This is the first of hopefully many opportunities that David will have to contribute to a book.

More information can be found on his website: `http://www.tookitaway.co.uk/`.

> As always, I'd like to thank my parents and family, who managed to make me the person I am today. I'd also like to thank my marvellous and splendid friends, who are always there for me when I need them. Not forgetting the best of the business world, Business Systems and Computer Services, the giants of the public sector. Work, learn, play, and have fun. It's your intentions, attitude, and what you do with your opportunities that set you apart.

Ross Stone (MCITP, MCSA) is a Windows system administrator with many years of experience in deploying and managing Active Directory, Windows servers, and a wide range of Microsoft technologies.

He is currently working at the Victoria and Albert Museum in London and is responsible for managing the Active Directory and Windows infrastructure estate.

More information can be found on his website at `http://rossstone.net`.

Nisarg Vora is currently a senior at Penn State University, specializing in software design and development with a minor in security and risk analysis. He also works for Pennsylvania Department of Human Services, where he is responsible for server and database management as well as application development to manage Windows Active Directory by developing and integrating PowerShell scripts in C# applications.

Apart from his education and work, as a part of his current research project at Penn State University, he is developing a Google Glass application for first emergency responders to help them receive all necessary information with ease in emergency situations.

In his free time, he loves playing his favorite games online with his friends, and due to his interest in gaming as well as development, he has started developing a Unity platform-based 2D games for iOS. He currently has an online portfolio at http://nisargvora.com and plans to add a blog in the near future.

www.PacktPub.com

Support files, eBooks, discount offers, and more

For support files and downloads related to your book, please visit www.PacktPub.com.

Did you know that Packt offers eBook versions of every book published, with PDF and ePub files available? You can upgrade to the eBook version at www.PacktPub.com and as a print book customer, you are entitled to a discount on the eBook copy. Get in touch with us at service@packtpub.com for more details.

At www.PacktPub.com, you can also read a collection of free technical articles, sign up for a range of free newsletters and receive exclusive discounts and offers on Packt books and eBooks.

https://www2.packtpub.com/books/subscription/packtlib

Do you need instant solutions to your IT questions? PacktLib is Packt's online digital book library. Here, you can search, access, and read Packt's entire library of books.

Why subscribe?

- Fully searchable across every book published by Packt
- Copy and paste, print, and bookmark content
- On demand and accessible via a web browser

Free access for Packt account holders

If you have an account with Packt at www.PacktPub.com, you can use this to access PacktLib today and view 9 entirely free books. Simply use your login credentials for immediate access.

Instant updates on new Packt books

Get notified! Find out when new books are published by following @PacktEnterprise on Twitter or the *Packt Enterprise* Facebook page.

Table of Contents

Preface

This book is for IT professionals who manage the Windows Active Directory infrastructure. Professionals supporting the Active Directory infrastructure, operations teams, and help desk members will find the content of this book useful. Any experience in PowerShell would be beneficial to help you easily grasp the content. Also, beginners can use this book to learn how to manage Active Directory environment using PowerShell.

What this book covers

Chapter 1, Let's Get Started, gives you an overview of the components, software, and modules required to manage Active Directory with PowerShell and gets you kick-started with routine tasks for automation. It also gives you the directions you need to use this book.

Chapter 2, Managing User and Computer Objects, helps users to perform various user and computer account administration related activities using PowerShell. By the end of this chapter, you will have a good understanding of how to manage user and computer Active Directory accounts using PowerShell and perform some of the automations based on it.

Chapter 3, Working with Active Directory Groups and Memberships, focuses on creating, modifying, and querying various kinds of security groups in Active Directory and their memberships. This chapter delivers the skills which are necessary for managing security groups in the Active Directory environment using PowerShell.

Chapter 4, Configuring Group Policies, helps in creating, linking, and unlinking Group Policies at various scopes; also, it is an integral part of Active Directory. By the end of this chapter, you will learn how to create GPOs, link them, enforce them, and perform several other operations using PowerShell. You will also be able to determine what policies are applied to a user and computer, remotely.

Chapter 5, Managing Domains, Organizational Units, Sites, and Subnets, tells you how to manage domains, Organizational Units, sites, and IP subnets using PowerShell. After completing this chapter, you will know how to manage OUs, sites, and IP subnets in your Active Directory environment.

Chapter 6, Advanced AD Operations Using PowerShell, talks about performing some of the advanced operations in Active directory such as promoting and demoting Active Directory domain controllers, the recovery of AD objects, and working with replication using PowerShell. After completing this chapter, you will know how to perform advanced AD operations, which are essential for any Active Directory administrator in a large enterprise environment.

Chapter 7, Managing DFS-N and DFS-R Using PowerShell, demonstrates how to create, configure, and query Distributed File System Namespace (DFS-N) and Distributed File System Replication (DFS-R) using PowerShell. By the end of this chapter, you will know how to administer DFS-N and DFS-R in a complex environment with the help of PowerShell.

Chapter 8, Managing Active Directory DNS Using PowerShell, helps you to understand how to manage AD DNS servers using PowerShell. A variety of operations such as clearing cache, creating and modifying records, working with zones, and many similar operations are covered in this chapter. By the end of this chapter, you will be able manage Active Directory DNS servers using PowerShell to create, modify, and delete records, and perform some of the advanced DNS server operations.

Chapter 9, Miscellaneous Scripts and Resources for Further Learning, gives the information which you need about managing Active Directory using PowerShell. This will also provide references and code samples for some of the frequently performed Active Directory operations. By the end of this chapter, you will know where to look for further help.

What you need for this book

This book is written to demonstrate the management of Active Directory in the Windows Server 2012 R2 environment. While all code samples provided here work in the Windows Server 2012 R2 environment, some will work in Windows Server 2008 R2 and Windows Server 2012 environments as well. The system and services that are required to work on are as follows:

- PowerShell v3 or later
- Windows Server 2012 R2 with the following roles installed:
    - Active Directory
    - Domain Naming System (DNS) server

  ○   Distributed File System Namespace (DFS-N)

  ○   Distributed File System Replication (DFS-R)

Who this book is for

If you are looking to automate the repetitive tasks in Active Directory management using the PowerShell module, then this book is for you. Any experience in PowerShell would be an added advantage.

Conventions

In this book, you will find a number of styles of text that distinguish between different kinds of information. Here are some examples of these styles, and an explanation of their meaning.

Code words in text, database table names, folder names, filenames, file extensions, pathnames, dummy URLs, user input, and Twitter handles are shown as follows: "The Get-ADUser command can be used to query user information. We can apply filters to narrow down the results using the -Filter and -LDAPFilter parameters".

A block of code is set as follows:

```
function Get-ADObjectsCount {
[CmdletBinding()]
param(
)
$Users = Get-ADUser -Filter *
$Groups = Get-ADGroup -Filter *
$Computers = Get-ADComputer -Filter *
$DomainName = (Get-ADDomain).Name
"{0} Users, {1} Computers and {2} Groups found in {3} Domain" -f
$Users.Count,$Computers.Count,$Groups.Count,$DomainName
}
```

Any command-line input or output is written as follows:

```
PS C:\> Get-ADObjectsCount
110 Users, 13 Computers and 83 Groups found in techibee Domain


PS C:\>
```

New terms and **important words** are shown in bold. Words that you see on the screen, in menus or dialog boxes, for example, appear in the text like this: "add the **Group Policy Management** option to install this feature".

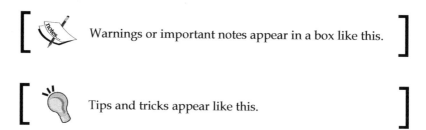

Warnings or important notes appear in a box like this.

Tips and tricks appear like this.

Reader feedback

Feedback from our readers is always welcome. Let us know what you think about this book—what you liked or may have disliked. Reader feedback is important for us to develop titles that you really get the most out of.

To send us general feedback, simply send an e-mail to feedback@packtpub.com, and mention the book title via the subject of your message.

If there is a topic that you have expertise in and you are interested in either writing or contributing to a book, see our author guide on www.packtpub.com/authors.

Customer support

Now that you are the proud owner of a Packt book, we have a number of things to help you to get the most from your purchase.

Downloading the example code

You can download the example code files for all Packt books you have purchased from your account at http://www.packtpub.com. If you purchased this book elsewhere, you can visit http://www.packtpub.com/support and register to have the files e-mailed directly to you.

Errata

Although we have taken every care to ensure the accuracy of our content, mistakes do happen. If you find a mistake in one of our books—maybe a mistake in the text or the code—we would be grateful if you would report this to us. By doing so, you can save other readers from frustration and help us improve subsequent versions of this book. If you find any errata, please report them by visiting http://www.packtpub.com/submit-errata, selecting your book, clicking on the **errata submission form** link, and entering the details of your errata. Once your errata are verified, your submission will be accepted and the errata will be uploaded on our website, or added to any list of existing errata, under the Errata section of that title. Any existing errata can be viewed by selecting your title from http://www.packtpub.com/support.

Piracy

Piracy of copyright material on the Internet is an ongoing problem across all media. At Packt, we take the protection of our copyright and licenses very seriously. If you come across any illegal copies of our works, in any form, on the Internet, please provide us with the location address or website name immediately so that we can pursue a remedy.

Please contact us at copyright@packtpub.com with a link to the suspected pirated material.

We appreciate your help in protecting our authors, and our ability to bring you valuable content.

Questions

You can contact us at questions@packtpub.com if you are having a problem with any aspect of the book, and we will do our best to address it.

Let's Get Started

1

Welcome to managing Active Directory using PowerShell. There are lot of good books from Packt Publishing that you might want to refer to improve your PowerShell skills. Assuming that you know the basics of PowerShell, this book further helps you to manage Active Directory using PowerShell. Do not worry if you are not familiar with PowerShell. You can still make use of the content in this book because most of the one-liners quoted in this book are self-explanatory. This chapter will take you through some of the essential tools that are required for managing Active Directory using PowerShell:

- The Microsoft Active Directory PowerShell module
- The Quest Active Directory PowerShell module
- Native PowerShell cmdlets

Details of how to get these tools, install, and configure them are also provided in this chapter. The content in this book completely relies on these tools to query Active Directory, so it is important to install and configure them before you proceed with further chapters in this book.

Though you can install and use these tools on legacy operating systems such as Windows XP, Windows 7, Windows Server 2003, Windows Server 2003 R2, Windows Server 2008, Windows Server 2008 R2, and so on, we will focus mostly on using them on the latest versions of operating systems, such as Windows 8.1 and Windows Server 2012 R2. Most of the operations performed on Windows 8.1 and Windows Server 2012 work on its predecessors. Any noticeable differences will be highlighted as far as possible.

Another reason for using the latest versions of operating systems for demonstration is the features list that they provide. When the Microsoft Active Directory PowerShell module was initially introduced with Windows Server 2008 R2, it came with 76 cmdlets. In Windows Server 2012, the number of cmdlets increased from 76 to 135. Similarly, the Windows Server 2012 R2 release has 147 Active Directory cmdlets. Looking at this pattern, it is clear that Microsoft is focusing on bringing more and more functionality into the Active Directory PowerShell module with its new releases. This means the types of actions we can perform with the Microsoft Active Directory module are increasing. Because of these reasons, Windows 8.1 and Windows Server 2012 R2 are being used for demonstration so that you can learn more about managing Active Directory using PowerShell.

To see how many cmdlets a module has, use the following commands once you have the Active Directory PowerShell module installed using the approach that is discussed later in this chapter:

```
Import-Module ActiveDirectory
```

First, import the Active Directory module in a PowerShell window. You will see a progress bar as shown in the following screenshot:

Once the module is imported, then you can run the following command to verify how many cmdlets Active Directory module has:

```
(Get-Command -Module ActiveDirectory).Count
```

As you can see in the following screenshot, there are 147 cmdlets available in Active Directory module on a Windows Server 2012 R2 server:

Ways to automate Active Directory operations

Active Directory operations can be automated in different ways. You can use C#, VB, command line tools (such as dsquery), VBScript, PowerShell, Perl, and so on. Since this book focuses on using PowerShell, let's examine the methodologies that are widely used to automate Active Directory operations using PowerShell.

There are three ways available to manage Active Directory using PowerShell. Each of these has its own advantages and operating environments:

- The Microsoft Active Directory module
- The Quest Active Directory PowerShell cmdlets
- The native method of PowerShell

Let's dig into each of these and understand a bit more in terms of how to install, configure, and use them.

The Microsoft Active Directory module

As the name indicates, this PowerShell module is developed and supported by Microsoft itself. This module contains a group of cmdlets that you can use to manage **Active Directory Domain Services (AD DS)** and **Active Directory Lightweight Directory Services (AD LDS)**. The Microsoft Active Directory module is introduced with the Windows Server 2008 R2 operating system and you need to have at least this version of OS to make use of the module. This module comes as an optional feature on Windows Server 2008 R2, Windows Server 2012, and Windows Server 2012 R2 and gets installed by default when you install the AD DS or AD LDS server roles, or when you promote them as domain controllers. You can have this module installed on Windows 7 or Windows 8 by installing the **Remote Server Administration Tools (RSAT)** feature.

This module works by querying Active Directory through a service called **Active Directory Web Services (ADWS)**, which is available in Windows Server 2008 R2 or later operating systems. This means your domain should have at least one domain controller with an operating system such as Windows Server 2008 R2 or above to make the module work.

Don't get disappointed if none of your domain controllers are upgraded to Windows Server 2008 R2. Microsoft has released a component called Active Directory Management Gateway Service that runs as the Windows Server 2008 R2 ADWS service and provides the same functionality on Windows Server 2003 or Windows Server 2008 domain controllers.

You can read more about ADWS and gateway service functionality at http://technet.microsoft.com/en-us/library/dd391908(v=ws.10).aspx

Installing Active Directory

As mentioned earlier, if you promote a Windows Server 2008 R2 or later operating system to domain controller, there is no need to install this module explicitly. It comes with the domain controller installation process.

Installing Active Directory module on Windows 7, Windows 8, and Windows 8.1 is a two-step process. First, we need to install the Remote Server Administration Tool (RSAT) kit for the respective operating system; then we enable the Active Directory module, which is part of RSAT, as a second step.

Installing the Remote Server Administration Tool kit

First, download the RSAT package from one of the following links based on your operating system and install it with administrative privileges:

- RSAT for Windows 8.1 http://www.microsoft.com/en-us/download/details.aspx?id=39296

- RSAT for Windows 8 http://www.microsoft.com/en-us/download/details.aspx?id=28972

- RSAT for Windows 7 with SP1 http://www.microsoft.com/en-us/download/details.aspx?id=7887

Installing the Active Directory module

Once the RSAT package is installed, you need to enable **Remote Server Administration Tools | Role Administration Tools | AD DS and AD LDS Tools | Active Directory module for Windows PowerShell** via the **Turn Windows features on or off** wizard that you will find in the Control Panel of the Windows 7 or Windows 8 operating systems.

To install Active Directory module on Windows Server 2008, Windows Server 2008 R2, and Windows Server 2012 member servers, there is no need to install additional components. They are already part of the available features and it's just a matter of adding the feature to the operating system. This can be done using PowerShell or a regular GUI approach.

If you want to enable this feature using PowerShell in the aforementioned server operating systems, then use the following commands:

```
Import-Module ServerManager
Add-WindowsFeature RSAT-AD-PowerShell
```

The RSAT package comes with the build on Windows Server 2008 R2 and Windows Server 2012. No need to install RSAT explicitly. The Server Manager PowerShell module in these operating systems contains the cmdlet, `Add-WindowsFeature`, which is used for installing features. In this case, we are installing Active Directory module for the Windows PowerShell feature in the AD DS and AD LDS tools.

If you want to perform this installation on remote servers, you can use the PSRemoting feature in PowerShell. This is the best approach if you want to deploy Active Directory module on all your servers in your environment.

This Active Directory module for Windows PowerShell can be installed using GUI interface as well. You need to use Server Manager to add **Active Directory Module for Windows PowerShell** using the **Add Roles and Features Wizard** as shown in following screenshot:

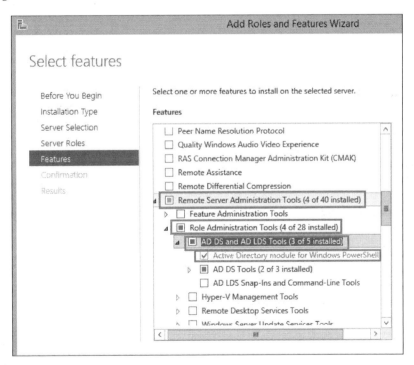

Testing the functionality

After installation, you can verify the functionality of Active Directory module by importing it and running a few basic cmdlets. A cmdlet is a simple command that is used in the Windows PowerShell environment. You can read more about cmdlets at `http://msdn.microsoft.com/en-us/library/ms714395(v=vs.85).aspx`.

Your installation is successful if you see your domain information after running the `Get-ADDomain` cmdlet, as shown in the following:

```
Import-Module ActiveDirectory

Get-ADDomain
```

> One good thing about PowerShell is you can avoid the hassle of typing the whole command in the PowerShell window by using the Tab Expansion feature. You can type part of the command and press the *Tab* key to autocomplete it. If there are multiple commands (or cmdlets) that match the string you typed, then use *Tab* multiple times to select the one you need. It's pretty handy because some of the cmdlets in Active Directory are considerably long and it can get really frustrating to type them. Refer to the TechNet page at `http://technet.microsoft.com/en-us/library/dd315316.aspx` in order to understand how you can use this feature of PowerShell.

Quest Active Directory PowerShell cmdlets

Previously, you learned that **Microsoft Active Directory (MS AD)** module was introduced with Windows Server 2008 R2. So, how did system administrators manage their Active Directory environments before the introduction of MS AD module? Quest Active Directory PowerShell cmdlets were present at that time to simplify AD operations. This Quest module has a bunch of cmdlets to perform various operations in Active Directory. Even after Microsoft released Active Directory module, many people still use Quest AD cmdlets because of its simplicity and the wide variety of management options it provides.

Quest AD module is part of the Quest ActiveRoles Server product, which is used for managing Active Directory objects. This Quest AD module is also referred to as ActiveRoles Management Shell for Active Directory because it is an integral part of the ActiveRoles product.

Installing Quest

Quest software (now acquired by Dell) allows you to download ActiveRoles Management Shell for free and you can download a copy from `https://support.software.dell.com/download-install-detail/5024645`. You will find two versions of Quest AD Management Shell in the download page. Be sure to download the latest one: v1.6.0.

While trying to install the MSI, you might get a prompt saying Microsoft .NET Framework 3.5 Service Pack 1 or later is required. You will experience this even if you have .NET framework 4.0 installed on your computer. It seems the MSI is specifically looking for .NET 3.5 SP1. So, ensure that you have .NET Framework 3.5 SP1 installed before you start installing the Quest AD management Shell MSI. You might want to refer to the TechNet article at `http://technet.microsoft.com/en-us/library/dn482071.aspx` to understand NET Framework 3.5 installation process on Windows Server 2012 R2.

After the completion of MSI, you can start using this module in two ways. You can either search in Program Files for the application with the name ActiveRoles Management Shell for Active Directory or you can add the Quest snap-in into the regular PowerShell window.

It's preferred to add the snap-in directly into existing PowerShell windows rather than opening a new Quest AD Shell when you want to manage Active Directory using Quest cmdlets. Also if you are authoring any scripts based on Quest AD cmdlets, it is best to add the snap-in in your code rather than asking the script users to run it from a Quest AD Shell window.

The Quest AD Snap-in can be added to an existing PowerShell window using the following command:

```
Add-PSSnapin Quest.ActiveRoles.ADManagement
```

After adding the snap-in, you can list the cmdlets provided by this snap-in using the following command:

```
Get-Command -Module Quest.ActiveRoles.ADManagement
```

`Get-Command` is the cmdlet used to list cmdlets or functions inside a given module or snap-in after importing them. The version (v1.6.0) of Quest AD Shell has 95 cmdlets. Unlike Microsoft Active Directory module, the number of cmdlets will not change from one operating system to another in Quest AD Shell. The list of cmdlets is the same irrespective of the operating system where the tool is installed.

One advantage of Quest AD Shell is that it doesn't need Active Directory Web services, which is mandatory for Microsoft Active Directory module. Quest AD Shell works with Windows Server 2003-based domain controllers as well without the need to install Active Directory Management Gateway Service.

Testing the functionality

Open a new PowerShell window and try the following commands.
The Get-QADRootDSE cmdlet should return your current domain information. All the Quest AD Shell cmdlets will have the word **QAD** prefixed to the noun:

```
Add-PSSnapin -Name Quest.ActiveRoles.ADManagement
```

```
Get-QADRootDSE
```

Using the Native method of PowerShell

Both Microsoft AD module and Quest AD module have a dependency and require additional software or components installed. If your environment cannot afford the installation of new components, then you are left with only one option to manage Active Directory using native PowerShell, which uses .NET classes. This doesn't require any extra components to be installed and the only thing required is .NET, which is present by default on any Windows operating system.

To query all computers in the current domain, use a query given in the following command:

```
([ADSISearcher]"Objectclass=Computer").Findall()
```

The example shown in the following screenshot might look simple but, as you need to do more with the native method approach, the complexity of the code will increase. Also, you will find less help from the community when querying Active Directory using the native method. Because of these reasons, Microsoft AD module or Quest module are preferred for easy Active Directory operations. Use this approach only if you have no other option.

```
PS C:\> ([ADSISearcher]"Objectclass=Computer").Findall()

Path                                                        Properties
----                                                        ----------
LDAP://CN=WIN-GUOPBL7NKSG,OU=Singapore,OU=LAB,DC=techibe... {ridsetreferences, logoncount, codepage, objectcategory...}
LDAP://CN=TIBDC2,OU=Domain Controllers,DC=techibee,DC=ad   {ridsetreferences, logoncount, codepage, objectcategory...}
LDAP://CN=TIB-WIN8PC,OU=Singapore,OU=LAB,DC=techibee,DC=ad {logoncount, codepage, objectcategory, description...}
LDAP://CN=SRVMEM1,CN=Computers,DC=techibee,DC=ad           {logoncount, codepage, objectcategory, iscriticalsystemo...

PS C:\>
```

Summary

In this chapter, you learned about the tools that the PowerShell module requires for managing Active Directory and how to get started with them. It is necessary to install these tools and modules in your environment to facilitate Active Directory operations using PowerShell.

Having these tools and modules in working condition is essential for practicing with the code samples provided throughout this book.

In the next chapter, you will learn in detail about how to manage user and computer Active Directory objects using PowerShell.

2
Managing User and Computer Objects

In the previous chapter, we got familiarized with a list of tools required for managing Active Directory using PowerShell. Now, let's get started with actual management tasks and feel the real power of automation. This chapter enables you to learn automation of a few user and computer account-related operations.

This chapter mainly focuses on accomplishing the following tasks using PowerShell:

- Creating new user and computer accounts
- Modifying user and computer objects
- Enabling or disabling user and computer accounts
- Moving user and computer accounts
- Deleting user and computer accounts

Managing user accounts

Active Directory is all about users and computers. Each user in the organization will have at least one account. There will be scenarios where a single user can have multiple accounts. This is very true in the case of IT users where one account is used for regular activities such as checking emails, browsing, and so on, whereas, the other privileged account is used for managing the infrastructure. Apart from this, there are service accounts that are designed to run a particular service. This shows how rapidly user accounts can grow in the Active Directory environment along with the necessity to manage them in a much more efficient way.

The following sections will explain how to perform user object operations using PowerShell.

Creating user accounts

Managing user accounts is one of the day-to-day jobs as a Windows administrator. New users join companies on a frequent basis and sometimes the volume might go high. In such cases, creating user accounts using conventional methods is time-consuming and prone to errors. So, relying on automation for creating new users would be a wise choice and less time-consuming.

In Active Directory, the manual account creation process involves **Graphical User Interface (GUI)** tools, such as **Active Directory Users and Computers (ADUC)** or **Active Directory Administrative Center (ADAC)**.

Let's first take a look at how user creation can be done using ADAC.

ADAC was first introduced in Windows Server 2008 R2. It relies on Active Directory PowerShell cmdlets in Windows Server 2008 R2 and uses them in the background to perform the Active Directory operations. ADAC is further enhanced in Windows Server 2012 to expose the PowerShell commands that it uses in the background and repays study.

The AD module can be loaded into a normal PowerShell window using the following command:

```
Import-Module ActiveDirectory
```

Ensure that you open your PowerShell window in the elevated mode (run as Administrator) to gain maximum benefits from the module.

Now, let's see the user creation process using a GUI tool named ADAC, shown in the following screenshot:

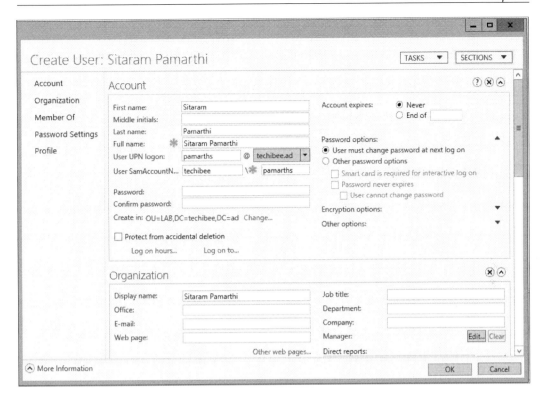

There are two mandatory fields that must be provided in order to create a user account: **Full Name** and **User SamAccountName**. Other fields are optional at the time of user creation and can be updated later. You might have also noticed that the password is not specified at the time of creation, so Active Directory keeps this field in a disabled state until the password is set. Once the password is set by the administrator, the user object has to be enabled explicitly.

Similarly, when a user account is created using PowerShell, it has one mandatory property that must be passed, the Name parameter. This parameter is equivalent to the **Full Name** value in UI. Also, the same parameter value is used for the user's **SamAccountName** attribute at the time of user account creation using PowerShell.

A user account in Active Directory can be created using the New-ADUser cmdlet. The following command is a small example to show how user account creation can be done:

```
New-ADUser -Name testuser1
```

When this command is executed from the PowerShell window, it creates a user account in the default user container. The account created will be in a disabled state because no password has been provided at the time of creation. This behavior is different when you create users using ADUC, where providing a password is mandatory.

The preceding one liner is just not sufficient for creating user accounts in the production environment. You are required to provide values for different attributes such as **First Name, Last Name, Display Name, Password options** (such as **User must change password at next logon** or not), **Office** address, phone numbers, **Job title, Department,** and the list goes on. So, we need to enhance our code to populate these properties at the time of login.

Before we start creating a full-fledged user account, let's see which properties can be populated by the New-ADUser cmdlet at the time of user creation. You can get this simply by running the following help command:

```
Get-Help New-ADUser -Detailed
```

The Get-Help cmdlet is the PowerShell cmdlet to see the help content of any other cmdlet. The usage of the -Detailed switch tells the Get-Help cmdlet to return all the help content for the given cmdlet. It includes a list of parameters, their syntax, an explanation of parameters, and examples.

To know more about each parameter, you can refer to the TechNet article at http:// technet.microsoft.com/en-us/library/ee617253.aspx. This TechNet article explains about data types that each parameter stores and this is important to understand in order to read and write the attributes.

> It is important to pay attention to the type of the value each parameter takes. If you provide any other data type apart from what it accepts, the New-ADUser cmdlet ends in an error. The type of information that each parameter takes can be identified from the TechNet page at http://technet.microsoft.com/en-us/library/ee617253.aspx.

As you can see in the preceding command, there are various properties (called attributes in AD terminology) that you can set at the time of user creation. If the attribute you want to set is not present, then you can use the OtherAttributes parameter to set it. Note that you need to provide other attribute names and values in hash table format while passing to the OtherAttributes parameter. Don't worry about the use of hash tables. It is clearly explained later in this chapter in the *Modifying user properties* section.

Now, let's see how we can create a user account by passing all kinds of values that we want to set at the time of user creation. This example will cover some of the properties that are frequently used at the time of user object creation. However, you can modify this command and play around with setting other parameters. Practice makes one perfect!!!

The `passthru` parameter is used to return the user object after creation of the account. If this parameter is not specified, the cmdlet will not show any output after successful creation of the object.

First, we need to prepare a password for the user to do the setting. Since the `-AccountPassword` cmdlet requires the input to be in secure string format, we need to populate the `$password` variable with the desired password, as shown by the following command:

```
$Password = Read-Host "Enter the password that you want to set" -
    AsSecureString
```

This will prompt you to enter the password and you will see asterisk symbols as you enter. Ensure that the password you enter should meet the password complexity of your domain, otherwise the following command will fail:

```
New-ADUser -Name Johnw -Surname "Williams" -GivenName "John" -
    EmailAddress "john.williams@techibee.ad" -SamAccountName "johnw" -
    AccountPassword $password -DisplayName "John Williams" -Department
    "Sales" -Country "US" -City "New York" -Path
    "OU=LAB,DC=Techibee,DC=AD" -Enabled $true -PassThru
```

Ensure that you update the `-Path` parameter in the preceding command to reflect the distinguished name of the OU in your environment. Otherwise, the operation might fail.

 Note: The `-Path` parameter is optional. If you don't specify this, the user account will be created in the default users container.

Executing the preceding command from PowerShell will return the output shown in the following screenshot:

The output shows the path of the object where it is created and other properties we set during the creation process. By default, the output shows only a minimum set of attributes. You can see all current attributes and the values of a user object using the the `Get-ADUser` cmdlet:

```
Get-ADUser -Identity JohnW -Properties *
```

Creating bulk user accounts

So far, we have seen how to create a single user account in Active Directory. Now, let's explore how to create multiple user accounts in one go.

The following command is sufficient enough if you want to create bulk user objects in the LAB environment without worrying about other properties such as department, email, and so on:

```
1..100 | foreach { New-ADUser -Name "Labuser$_" -AccountPassword
   $password -Path "OU=LAB,DC=techibee,DC=AD"}
```

It is a simple foreach loop that runs 100 times to create a user account with the name `Labuser` suffixed by the number of iteration (such as Labuser1, Labuser2, and so on.) with the password set to the value of the `$password` variable.

However, this is not sufficient to create user accounts in production environments. We need to populate several attributes at the time of creation. Ideally, system administrators receive the account creation information from HR in CSV format. So, the example being demonstrated in the following screenshot reads the account information from a CSV file, which has the details of user attributes, and creates user accounts based on this information.

	A	B	C	D	E	F	G	H
1	FirstName	LastName	Displayname	Email	LoginName	Country	City	
2	Dave	Williams	Dave Williams	Dave.Williams@techibee.com	DaveW	US	New York	
3	Chris	Brown	Chris Brown	Chris.Brown@techibee.ad	ChrisB	UK	London	
4	John	Miller	John Miller	John.Miller@techibee.ad	JohnM	US	Redmond	
5								

Let's first read the content of the CSV file into a PowerShell variable. A cmdlet called `Import-CSV` is available in PowerShell that can read the contents of the CSV file and return the output in object format. We can make use of it to read the contents, as shown in the following command:

```
$Users = Import-CSV <path of the saved CSV file>

$Users | Format-Table
```

This command will read the contents of the CSV file into the `$Users` variable. The next statement will show the contents of the variable in table format. It should look as follows:

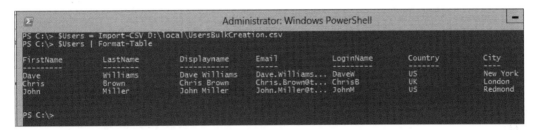

Now, we have all user details in a variable, so let's proceed to create user accounts:

```
foreach($User in $Users) {
New-ADUser -Name $User.LoginName -Surname $User.LastName -
   GivenName $User.FirstName -EmailAddress $User.Email -
   SamAccountName $User.LoginName -AccountPassword $Password -
   DisplayName $User.DisplayName -Country $User.Country -City
   $User.City -Path "OU=LAB,DC=Techibee,DC=AD" -Enabled $true -
   PassThru
}
```

The preceding code will loop through each object in the `$Users` variable and invoke creation of user accounts by passing the properties of the `$User` object to parameters of the `New-ADUser` cmdlet. The value of the -path parameter in code has been hardcoded here, but you can make it part of the CSV file and pass it using the `-Path` parameter during creation. Executing this code will create three accounts in Active Directory with the details given in the CSV file.

All you need to do is populate the CSV file with the details you want to apply to each user object and prepare the New-ADUser cmdlet accordingly. Refer to *Chapter 9, Miscellaneous Scripts and Resources for Further Learning* for a more enhanced version of bulk user creation script.

Modifying user properties

In the previous section, we have seen how to create user accounts using Active Directory PowerShell module. The task of the system administrator will not end by just creating user objects in Active Directory; he/she will also be responsible for modifying and managing them. This section will help you understand the process involved in modifying user accounts using PowerShell.

Since modifying user accounts has a very big scope, we will discuss a few example cases where a bulk user modification is required. These examples will help you understand the modification process. You can leverage these examples to modify any other attributes in Active Directory:

- Updating the description of a user object
- Updating the telephone number of multiple users
- Enabling or disabling user accounts in bulk
- Moving user accounts to another OU

Before jumping on to modifying user properties, let's brush up on the basics basics. To update the description of a user account, you will typically follow these steps:

1. Open the ADAC tool (or ADUC).
2. Search for a username in Active Directory.
3. Go to the properties of the object.
4. Update the description and save your changes by clicking on **OK**.

What happens under the hood when you update the description of the object and save it? The system writes the value to a respective attribute of that user object. You can view all attributes and their values using the **Attribute Editor** tab in ADAC (or ADUC in Windows Server 2008 R2). To view this information from Windows Server 2003, you need to use the adsiedit.msc tool.

Here are the attribute details of user objects we created during bulk user creation in the previous section. You can see the values that are being read from the CSV file and used for creation.

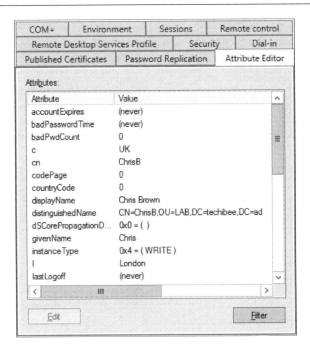

So, in order to update any details of a user object, first we need to know its attribute name or display name.

 Always remember that the names for properties you see in GUI tools might not be the same as what you see in the attribute editor. For example, the **First Name** field you see in GUI is translated to **givenName** in the attribute editor.

Similar to the GUI approach, we can search for a user object and list its attributes using PowerShell. The Get-ADUser cmdlet can be used for this:

```
Get-ADUser -Filter {Name -eq "ChrisB" }
```

This will return the user object with the Name attribute having the value ChrisB. By default, it will return only a basic set of attributes. If you want to see all attributes of this user object, then specify the -Property parameter, as shown in the following command:

```
Get-ADUser -Filter {Name -eq "ChrisB" } -Property *
```

You can also query users matching their name Chris by adjusting the value of the -Filter parameter, as shown in the following command:

```
Get-ADUser -Filter {Name -like "Chris*" }
```

Similarly, we can query all objects inside a particular Organizational Unit by passing the OU distinguished name to the `-SearchBase` parameter, as shown in the following command:

```
Get-ADUser -Filter * -SearchBase "OU=LAB,dc=techibee,dc=ad"
```

Now that we know how to search for objects, let's move on to learn how to modify them.

Updating the description of a user object

In the previous section, you learned how to search and find a user object. Let's use that logic and get an instance of the `ChrisB` user object, as shown in the following command:

```
$UserObj = Get-ADUser -Filter {Name -eq "ChrisB" } -Properties *
```

The `$UserObj` variable stores the reference to the `ChrisB` user object. We can view the current description of the user object by using the following command, assuming the user account has a description set:

```
$UserObj.Description
```

To replace the current description with new value, first we need to understand what data type this attribute will accept. As we mentioned before, we can find this out using the `GetType()` method. You can invoke this method, as shown in the following command:

```
$userObj.Description.GetType()
```

The output of this command shows that it accepts data of `string`, as shown in the following screenshot:

```
PS C:\> $userObj.Description.GetType()

IsPublic IsSerial Name                                     BaseType
-------- -------- ----                                     --------
True     True     String                                   System.Object

PS C:\>
```

To update the description to a new value, we need to use the `Set-ADuser` cmdlet and pass the `$UserObj` to the `-Identity` parameter and the string that you want to set in the description field to the `-Description` parameter. The following command will return to the PS prompt in the PowerShell window if it completes without any errors:

```
Set-ADUser -Identity $UserObj -Description "Added new description via
   PowerShell"
```

To verify if the new description is updated in the user description field, we can either check it through the GUI or run the PowerShell command that we used for querying the user object in the preceding command.

Putting everything together, the following code will update the description of a given Active Directory user:

```
$UserName = "ChrisB"
$NewDescription = "Delete this account after November"
$UserObj = Get-ADUser -Filter {Name -eq $UserName} -Properties *
Write-Host "Current description is : $($UserObj.Description)"
Set-ADUser -Identity $UserObj -Description $NewDescription
$UserObj = Get-ADUser -Filter {Name -eq $UserName} -Properties *
Write-Host "New description is : $($UserObj.Description)"
```

Downloading the example code

You can download the example code files for all Packt books you have purchased from your account at http://www.packtpub.com. If you purchased this book elsewhere, you can visit http://www.packtpub.com/support and register to have the files e-mailed directly to you.

You can update values of any other attribute using the procedure explained in this code. As a matter of practice, try updating the DisplayName of a user.

Remember? Practice makes perfect!!!

Updating the telephone numbers of multiple users

In the previous example, you learned how to update the value of description using PowerShell. Now, let's take a look at updating telephone numbers of multiple users. This operation is a little different from updating the description operation. Here, we have two complexities, which are as follows:

1. We don't know which attribute will get updated when a number is added to the telephone number field in the GUI.

2. Performing a telephone number update for multiple users by reading from a text file or CSV file.

Let's address these complexities one by one. First, we need to identify attributes that need to be updated. In this demonstration, we want to update the **Office** telephone number, **Home** number, and **mobile** number of the users. If these users already have these numbers set, then we can use the attribute editor to identify the attribute names that need to be updated. If not, set these telephone numbers for one user account and then use attribute editor to identify the attribute names. Alternatively, you can use the `Get-ADUser` cmdlet to retrieve all attributes. The PowerShell way is preferred here, as we want to learn more and more about it. Examine the output of the following command carefully and identify the attribute names that have the telephone numbers you see in the GUI:

```
Get-ADUser -Identity chrisB -Properties *
```

You will notice that the following command has the telephone numbers you see in the GUI:

```
Get-ADUser -Identity ChrisB -Properties * | select HomePhone,
    OfficePhone, mobile
```

The description of the preceding command is shown in the following:

- `OfficePhone`: This attribute contains the phone number that you see under the **Main** field in telephone numbers in ADAC. In ADUC, you will see this number in the **Telephone number** field in the **General** tab.
- `HomePhone`: This is the phone number you will see in the **Home Phone** field.
- `mobile`: This attribute contains the phone number you will see in the **Mobile** field.

First, let's update the telephone details of one user, then we can extend the logic to update other users in bulk.

Let's store the numbers in variables first, as shown in the following commands:

```
$OfficeNumber = "+65 12345678"

$HomeNumber = "+65 87654321"

$MobileNumber = "+65 13578642"
```

The next step is to update the preceding values for a user account, as shown in the following command:

```
Set-ADUser -Identity ChrisB -OfficePhone $OfficeNumber -HomePhone
    $HomeNumber -MobilePhone $MobileNumber
```

This is straightforward because the `Set-ADUser` cmdlet has parameters that can set these phone numbers. If the attribute that you are trying to set is not available as a parameter to the cmdlet then you can use the `-Add` parameter to directly specify the attribute name and the value. Similarly, you can use other parameters such as `-Replace` and `-Clear` to work with attributes directly. The preceding example can be rewritten using the `-Add` parameter, as shown in the following commands:

```
Set-ADUser -Identity ChrisB -Clear telephonenumber, homephone, mobile
Set-ADUser -Identity ChrisB -Add @{telephonenumber = $OfficeNumber;
  homephone = $HomeNumber ; mobile = $MobileNumber }
```

Here, we are setting the office phone number to the `telephonenumber` attribute, the home number to the `homephone` attribute, and the mobile number to the `mobile` attribute. Before setting them, we will clear existing values using the `-Clear` parameter.

Now, we can extend this logic to multiple users using a for loop in PowerShell. Before doing this, store the user names and numbers you want to set in a CSV file and import it into PowerShell. The following screenshot shows how the contents of the CSV look:

	A	B	C	D	E
1	UserName	OfficeNumber	HomeNumber	MobileNumber	
2	ChrisB	+65 12345678	+65 87654321	+65 13578642	
3	SteveR	+65 12345678	+65 97054367	+65 43561209	
4					
5					
6					

And the code to set the telephone numbers is as follows:

```
$Users = Import-CSV c:\temp\usersPhoneNumbers.csv
foreach($User in $Users) {
Set-ADUser -Identity $User.UserName -OfficePhone $User.OfficeNumber
-HomePhone $User.HomeNumber -MobilePhone $User.MobileNumber
}
```

Enabling or disabling user accounts

Now, let's take a look at another scenario where we want to perform bulk user enable/disable operation. Fortunately, there are two cmdlets provided in Active Directory module to make this operation very easy and straightforward.

They are as follows:

- `Enable-ADAccount`: This cmdlet is used for enabling Active Directory user, computer, or service account objects
- `Disable-ADAccount`: This cmdlet is used for disabling Active Directory user, computer, or service account objects

Both these cmdlets require an object to be enabled/disabled. The object can be in one of the following formats:

- Distinguished Name (DN) format, for example, CN=ChrisB, OU=LAB, DC=techibee, and DC=ad
- ObjectGUID format, for example, 923199de-0dd9-4758-a954-5aa42409b10d
- Security Identifier (SID) format, for example S-1-5-21-822638036-2026389545-1116158610-1244
- `SAMAccountName` format, for example, ChrisB

To get these values for a given user, use the `Get-ADUser` cmdlet (use `Get-ADComputer` in the case of computer accounts)

Now, it's just a matter of passing the input values to either the `Enable-ADAccount` or `Disable-ADAccount` cmdlets based on which operation you want to perform.

Here are some common usage scenarios. These scenarios cover disable operations; to perform enable operations in a similar way, just replace the `Disable-ADAccount` cmdlet with the `Enable-ADAccount` cmdlet.

The following command can be used to disable a single user account:

```
Disable-ADAccount -Identity ChrisB -Passthru
```

The `-PassThru` parameter is used to return the object after the completion of the operation. Also it is useful to know the disable status if you want to perform further actions on this object.

You can disable users in a particular OU. The following command will return all users objects under LAB OU and its sub OUs:

```
Get-ADUser -SearchBase "OU=LAB,DC=techibee,DC=AD" -Filter * |
  Disable-ADAccount
```

To limit the search scope to the current OU, use the `-SearchScope` parameter. It takes three values: Basic (or 0), OneLevel (or 1), a Subtree (or 2). Subtree is the default value when nothing is specified.

Read usernames from a text file and disable them, as shown in the following command:

```
Get-Content C:\temp\users.txt | % { Disable-ADAccount -Identity $_ }
```

Here, the `Get-Content` cmdlet reads the usernames from the text file and passes them one by one to the `Disable-ADAccount` cmdlet using a foreach loop (`%` is an alias for a foreach loop in PowerShell). When passing the user name to the `Disable-ADAccount` cmdlet, we use the `$_` automatic variable, which contains the name that is passed from the pipeline. Read more about automatic variables at `http://technet.microsoft.com/en-us/library/hh847768.aspx`.

You can disable all users in a department, for example, Sales. The following command queries all users who have their department value set to `sales` and passes them to the `Disable-ADAccount` cmdlet to disable them:

```
Get-ADUser -Filter 'Department -eq "sales"' | Disable-ADAccount
```

Likewise, to perform an enable operation, just replace `Disable-ADAccount` with the `Enable-ADAccount` cmdlet in the preceding examples.

Moving user accounts to another OU

For example, let's consider a scenario where all users of one department are moved from one office building to another. So, you would like to move all these user accounts to a new OU for ease of identification and management.

The `Move-ADObject` cmdlet is available in Active Directory module to accomplish this operation. As you might have already noted, this particular cmdlet can move any object from one OU to another; not just user accounts.

This cmdlet has two mandatory parameters:

- `Identity`: This identifies the object that you want to move. It can be either the Distinguished name (DN) of the object or the GUID of the object.

- `TargetPath`: The `TargetPath` parameter must be the Distinguished Name (DN) of OU or the container to which you want to move the objects.

Here are some use case scenarios:

- Moving a user account from one OU to another:

  ```
  Move-ADObject -Identity "CN=ChrisB,OU=LAB,DC=techibee,DC=ad" -
      TargetPath "OU=Singapore,OU=LAB,DC=Techibee,DC=ad"
  ```

  Here, `ChrisB` is the name of the user that we are moving from the current location (specified in the DN) to the new `-TargetPath` parameter.

- Moving all users from LAB OU to PROD OU

```
Get-ADUser -Filter * -SearchBase "OU=LAB,DC=techibee,DC=ad" |
  Move-ADObject -TargetPath "OU=Prod,DC=techibee,DC=ad"
```

The preceding command will move all users (including users in sub OUs) from LAB OU to PROD OU. The `-Identity` parameter is automatically populated from the output of the `Get-ADUser` cmdlet.

You can use the following command to move users from one OU to another based on their department name:

```
Get-ADUser -Filter 'department -eq "Sales"' | Move-ADObject -TargetPath
"OU=Sales,OU=PROD,DC=techibee,DC=AD"
```

> Remember: The target OU must exist before you move users to it.
>
> The distinguished name of an object should always be unique; the common name portion of the distinguished name can, however, be used more than once.

Deleting user accounts

The Active Directory PowerShell module has a cmdlet called `Remove-ADUser` to delete user accounts from Active Directory. Alternatively, the `Remove-ADObject` cmdlet can be used. The `Remove-ADUser` cmdlet is designed to deal with user accounts removal. We will use this cmdlet throughout the examples in this section.

The requests for removal of user accounts increase as the attrition rate increases in your organization. You get requests from HR to delete user accounts on a frequent basis either when an employee leaves the organization or he/she turns down the offer just before joining.

> Most organizations won't delete user accounts when an employee leaves the organization. Instead, they will hide these from the **Global Address List/Book (GAL)**, remove them from all groups, disable the mailbox, and keep the ID in a disabled state. Such accounts can be enabled if the employee rejoins the company later.

Removing a user account from Active Directory is a straightforward process. You just need to pass the DN or ObjectGUID, SID or SamAccountName to the `-Identity` parameter of the `Remove-ADUser` cmdlet. In the following example, `Samaccountname` is passed to the `-Identity` parameter, as shown in the following command:

```
Remove-ADUser -Identity ChrisB
```

When this command is executed, it will ask for confirmation of deletion, as shown in the following screenshot:

```
Administrator: Windows PowerShell

PS C:\> Remove-ADUser -Identity ChrisB

Confirm
Are you sure you want to perform this action?
Performing operation "Remove" on Target "CN=ChrisB,OU=Sales,OU=Prod,DC=techibee,DC=ad".
[Y] Yes  [A] Yes to All  [N] No  [L] No to All  [S] Suspend  [?] Help (default is "Y"): Y
```

Since deletion is a critical operation, Active Directory module warns about it. If you are certain that the inputs are correct and you don't want to get prompted for confirmation, set the -Confirm parameter value to $false, as shown in the following command:

```
Remove-ADUser -Identity ChrisB -Confirm:$false
```

Similarly, to delete user accounts by reading from a text file, use the following command:

```
Get-Content C:\temp\users.txt | % { Remove-ADUser -Identity $_ -
  Confirm:$false}
```

The Get-Content cmdlet reads the usernames from users.txt and passes them to the Remove-ADUser cmdlet to delete the accounts one after another.

Managing computer accounts

In previous sections, we have seen several operational tasks that can be performed on user accounts in Active Directory using PowerShell. This section focuses on performing similar operations on computer objects.

Managing computer objects is not much different from managing user objects. All you need to do is to use the correct cmdlets and the rest of the process remains the same.

The following topics are covered as a part of managing computer accounts using PowerShell. Let's go through these one by one and understand how we can accomplish them:

- Creating computer accounts
- Modifying computer properties
- Enabling or disabling computer accounts
- Deleting computer accounts

Creating computer accounts

Most system administrators do not create computer accounts manually in Active Directory. Instead, they join computers to the domain and the account gets created automatically. After automatic object creation, the administrator moves the computer accounts from the default container to the desired OU.

Well, this might look quite simple but why is there a need to create a manual computer account? The aforementioned approach will work for small organizations where one set of system administrators will manage everything and they will have all privileges. However, in large organizations, this is not feasible for various reasons. In large organizations the desktop/server builds happen in an automated way using deployment solutions, such as **Windows Development Services (WDS)** where the build process looks for a computer account in AD to join the server/ desktop to the domain. This process is called prestaging of computer accounts and it has a good set of advantages such as choosing the OU where you want to place the computer, group membership, and so on.

So, let's now look at a few examples of creating a computer account. Active Directory provides a cmdlet called New-ADComputer to facilitate the computer account creation.

The following command will create a computer account with the name SRVMEM2 in the default computers container:

```
New-ADComputer -Name SRVMEM2 -PassThru
```

To create computer account in a particular Organizational Unit in Active Directory, use the following command:

```
New-ADComputer -Name SRVMEM2 -Path
  "OU=Computers,OU=PROD,DC=techibee,DC=AD" -PassThru
```

Ensure that the OU mentioned in the preceding command exists prior to the computer account creation; if not, the command execution fails.

If you just want to create the computer account but keep it in a disabled state, the following command helps:

```
New-ADComputer -Name SRVMEM2 -Path
  "OU=Computers,OU=PROD,DC=techibee,DC=AD" -Enabled $false -PassThru
```

 Notice: The -Enable parameter in the preceding command, which is set to $false, is responsible for disabling the computer account.

To see the list of other options for this cmdlet and some examples, read its complete help content. This can done using the following command:

```
Get-Help New-ADComputer -Full
```

Modifying computer accounts

Computer account attributes often need to be modified. For example, because many computer accounts are created before the computers are actually assigned to users, attributes such as description, department, and location cannot be configured at the time an account is created. In addition, the ownership of a computer can be transferred to a new user or department, or a computer might be physically moved to a new location. In such circumstances, the computer account attributes need to be modified.

Let's see the PowerShell way of doing this using various cmdlets available for computer objects.

Setting the description for a computer account

Active Directory PowerShell module has the Set-ADComputer cmdlet for modifying computer account properties in Active Directory. Remember the Set-ADUser cmdlet we used for modifying user object properties? It is similar to that but for computer accounts.

To update the description of a single computer, you can use the following command. This example updates the description of the SRVMEM1 computer object:

```
Set-ADComputer –identity SRVMEM1 –description "Member Server"
```

The Set-ADComputer cmdlet has ability to set values for the majority of object attributes. To see the list of attributes it can set, check its help content using the following command:

```
Get-Help Set-ADComputer -Full
```

You can use the `Get-ADComputer` command to check if the description is set as shown in the following screenshot:

```
Administrator: Windows PowerShell

PS C:\Users\Administrator> get-adcomputer SRVMEM1 -property description

Description       : Member Server
DistinguishedName : CN=SRVMEM1,CN=Computers,DC=techibee,DC=ad
DNSHostName       : SRVMEM1.techibee.ad
Enabled           : True
Name              : SRVMEM1
ObjectClass       : computer
ObjectGUID        : 1174644f-af0b-4995-9c1f-a72cacd79546
SamAccountName    : SRVMEM1$
SID               : S-1-5-21-822638036-2026389545-1116158610-1111
UserPrincipalName :
```

Moving computer accounts to a different OU

Sometimes, you might need to move computer accounts to different OUs as the user might change the location or server accounts in order to segregate them according to their roles; or you might want to move computer accounts from the default OU to respective office location OUs.

Let's see a few of the examples related to computer account movements across Organizational Units. As we have done for user accounts, here too we can make use of the `Move-ADObject` cmdlet to move computer accounts from one OU to another. The following command moves the SRVMEM1 computer account from the default computer container to Computers OU inside PROD OU:

```
Move-ADObject -Identity "CN=SRVMEM1,CN=Computers,DC=techibee,DC=ad" -
  TargetPath "OU=Computers,OU=PROD,DC=techibee,DC=ad" -PassThru
```

Since it is not possible to provide the full DN of the object we want to move every time, we can either use the `Get-ADComputer` or `Search-ADAccount` cmdlet to search by its name or some other property and then pass the output to the `Move-ADObject` cmdlet. The following example demonstrates this:

```
Get-ADComputer -Filter "name -eq 'SRVMEM1'" | Move-ADObject -
  TargetPath "OU=Computers,OU=PROD,DC=techibee,DC=ad" -PassThru
```

Similarly, we search for a string in the description of the computer objects and move them to the designated OU using the following command:

```
Get-ADComputer -Filter "description -like '*server*'" | Move-ADObject
-TargetPath "OU=Computers,OU=PROD,DC=techibee,DC=ad" -PassThru
```

This command will look for computer accounts that have the string server in their description and will move them to the designated OU. Similarly, you can search based on any other criteria and move them to different OUs, as shown in the preceding command.

Enabling or disabling computer accounts

As a system administrator, it is required to keep your Active Directory database clean, tidy, and minimal in size. Also, one must adhere to the security policies of the organization and often needs to reconcile computer accounts data monthly, quarterly, and annually in accordance with those security policies.

The cmdlet we use here is not specific to computer objects; it can also be used for any Active Directory user, computer, or service accounts.

Use the following command to enable a particular computer:

```
Get-ADComputer -Identity COMP1 | Enable-ADAccount
```

To enable multiple computer accounts, you can use filters in conjunction with the `Get-ADComputer` or `Search-ADAccount` cmdlets. The following command will search for computer accounts inside the given OU and it will enable all of them:

```
Get-ADComputer -Filter "*" -SearchBase
  "OU=Computers,OU=PROD,DC=techibee,DC=ad" | Enable-ADAccount -
  PassThru
```

Similarly, to disable computer accounts, just replace `Enable-ADAccount` with the `Disable-ADAccount` cmdlet. The following command disables all of the computers inside the given OU:

```
Get-ADComputer -Filter "*" -SearchBase
  "OU=Computers,OU=PROD,DC=techibee,DC=ad" | Disable-ADAccount -
  PassThru
```

Explore more by referring to the help content of these cmdlets. For example, to see the help of the `Get-ADComputer` cmdlet, you can use the following command:

```
Get-Help Get-ADComputer -Detailed
```

You can read the help content from TechNet site as well (http://technet. microsoft.com/en-us/library/ee617192.aspx).

Deleting computer accounts

As discussed in the previous section, as a system administrator one must adhere to the security policies of the organization and keep their Active Directory database clean and tidy. As part of this process, you might want to delete stale/offline computer objects from Active Directory.

Use the following simple command to delete a computer account:

```
Remove-ADComputer -Identity COMP1
```

The most common use case is searching for computers older than *x* days and removing them. You can achieve this using the following command:

```
$Computers = Get-ADComputer -Filter * -Properties LastLogonDate | ?
  {$_.LastLogonDate -lt (get-date).Adddays(-10) }

$Computers | Remove-ADComputer
```

> You need to be very careful while performing the delete operation. Any mistake in the filters can result in your production computers being deleted. So, I prefer storing the Get-ADComputer cmdlet results in a variable ($computer in this example), reviewing the list, and then passing it to the Remove-ADComputer cmdlet.

The first line in the preceding code searches Active Directory for computers that are not contacted in the last 30 days and stores them in a variable. Later, we can pass the variable to the Remove-ADComputer cmdlet to delete them. By default, this cmdlet will prompt for each deletion; you can override it using the -Confirm:$false property with the Remove-ADComputer cmdlet.

To delete multiple computer accounts that have location value set to OFFICE1, you can use the following command:

```
Get-ADComputer -filter 'Location -eq "OFFICE1"' | Remove-ADComputer -
  confirm:$false
```

Use the following command to delete all computer accounts in a particular OU:

```
Get-ADComputer -SearchBase "OU=DisabledComp,DC=techibee,DC=ad" |
  Remove-ADComputer -confirm:$false
```

These examples will help you to get started. For instance, you can use the `Get-ADComputer` cmdlet to search computer accounts using different patterns and pass them to the `Remove-ADComputer` cmdlet to delete them.

 Deletion of user accounts or computer accounts is a critical operation and reverting these changes is not possible in all cases. So, you should verify what you are searching and removing. Review the output of the `Get-ADComputer` cmdlet twice before you pass it to the `Remove-ADComputer` cmdlet.

Summary

In this chapter, we have seen how to manage Active Directory users and computer accounts using PowerShell. The examples quoted in each section will help you to get started. You can enhance your learning further by reviewing the help content of each cmdlet that we have used throughout this chapter.

You might wonder why managing group membership of users and computers is not covered in this chapter. Considering the fact that group membership changes are more frequent in Active Directory environment, the next chapter focuses in depth on this topic. Various operations related to groups and their memberships are covered there in great detail.

3

Working with Active Directory Groups and Memberships

In the previous chapter, you learned about managing user and computer objects using PowerShell. Now let's discuss how to manage Active Directory groups and their memberships.

In this chapter, we will see how to perform the following operations in Active Directory using PowerShell cmdlets:

- Creating local, global, and universal security groups
- Searching and modifying group object information
- Adding group members, user and computer accounts to the security groups
- Listing members of a security group in Active Directory
- Removing user or computer accounts from groups
- Removing a groups from groups
- Deleting or removing the AD groups

To start with, let's recollect some basic concepts about Active Directory groups and their memberships.

What is a group? A group is a collection of different Active Directory objects such as user accounts, computer accounts, and groups. Active Directory groups are basically categorized into two types: **Security groups** and **Distribution Lists/Groups (DL)**. A security group can be used to grant permissions to various resources in a network such as granting permissions to shares, **New Technology File System (NTFS)** permissions, printer permissions, and many more similar activities. DL is an e-mail-enabled group, using which information can be shared via e-mail to a group of people simultaneously. Security groups can be mail-enabled and used as a DL and vice versa.

Both of these groups are further characterized by a scope that identifies the extent to which the group is applied in a domain tree or forest. This means that the scope of a group determines whether it can have members from the same domain, different domains, or different forests. There are three types of scope available in Active Directory that apply to both of these groups. They are universal, global, and domain local.

> Note that, because distribution groups are used for e-mail and most importantly for Microsoft Exchange applications, we are limiting our discussion to security groups in this chapter. The approaches described in this article are applicable for distribution group as well. However, the PowerShell cmdlets provided by Microsoft Exchange application are more suitable to manage distribution groups. You may want to refer to group cmdlets mentioned on the TechNet page available at `http://technet.microsoft.com/en-us/library/bb124233%28v=exchg.150%29.aspx`.

In a Windows environment, Active Directory security groups play an important role. Using groups to delegate/grant permissions is very scalable compared to granting permissions to an individual user or computer account. Given these reasons, the number of group membership changes made in any organization on a day-to-day basis is very high. Since it is one of the tedious tasks every Windows system administrator has to perform on a daily basis, it is important to understand how to automate it to its maximum extent.

Creating different types of security groups

As mentioned before, there are different types of security groups available in Active Directory: global, domain local, and universal. You may refer to the TechNet article at `http://technet.microsoft.com/en-us/library/cc755692(v=ws.10).aspx` to know more about group scopes.

To create a new group in Active Directory, the `New-ADGroup` cmdlet can be used. This cmdlet accepts three parameters. These are `name` of the group, the Organizational Unit `path` in AD, and `groupScope`, such as domain local/global/ universal. Of these, `name` and `groupScope` need to be provided mandatorily.

Here is the simple command line to create a new blank AD group in AD with no members in it.

The following command creates a new Active Directory group of type `DomainLocal` in the specified OU:

```
New-ADGroup -Name "Test Group1" -Path
  "OU=Groups,OU=Prod,DC=techibee,DC=ad" -groupScope domainlocal
```

Similarly, to create other group types, change the parameter `-groupScope`. The following sample command creates a global group and a universal group:

```
New-ADGroup -Name "Test Group Global" -Path
  "OU=Groups,OU=Prod,DC=techibee,DC=ad" -groupScope global

New-ADgroup -Name "Test Group Universal" -Path
  "OU=Groups,OU=Prod,DC=techibee,DC=ad" -groupScope universal
```

 Note that we just modified the `groupScope` parameter details and rest of the command line remains the same. The name of the group can be anything of your choice.

Searching and modifying group object information

Searching Active Directory for the presence of a group is similar to searching users and groups. A cmdlet called `Get-ADGroup` from the Active Directory module can be used to get group object information.

For example, we can use the following command to get display names of all groups in Active Directory:

```
Get-ADGroup -Filter * | select Name
```

By specifying asterisk (*) as an argument to the `-Filter` parameter, we are querying all groups in Active Directory and then displaying the value of the `Name` property using the `select` statement.

To search for a specific group by name, we can pass the name of the group to the `-Filter` parameter, as shown in the following command:

```
Get-ADGroup -Filter "Name -eq 'Test Group1'"
```

This command searches Active Directory for groups with the name that exactly matches `Test Group1` and returns the group object if present; otherwise, no output is seen.

There is another parameter that helps in performing the search operation in Active Directory, that is, the `-LDAPFilter` parameter. The `-Filter` and `-LDAPFilter` parameters perform the same type of search operation but the syntax in which you pass the values is different. The `-Filter` parameter takes the PowerShell type of syntax and `-LDAPFilter` takes the LDAP type of syntax. The example command shown in the preceding command was written using the `-Filter` parameter, which uses the PowerShell syntax. The same command can be rewritten using `-LDAPFilter` as shown in the following command:

```
Get-ADGroup -LDAPFilter "(Name=Test Group1)"
```

Based on your comfort level, you can use either the `-Filter` or `-LDAPFilter` parameter to perform searches. This is applicable for other cmdlets such as the `Get-ADUser` and `Get-ADComputer` parameters. Another difference to note here is that `-Filter` can take the property names returned by cmdlets in the ActiveDirectory module but the `-LDAPFilter` parameter requires the exact attribute names.

> In general, using the `-Filter` parameter to perform search operations is sufficient. The `-LDAPFilter` parameter can be used to test the existing LDAP filters or the filters used in other programming languages that query Active Directory using LDAP.

You can read more about AD filters at the following TechNet page:

`http://technet.microsoft.com/en-us/library/`
`hh531527%28v=ws.10%29.aspx`

Also, there are a couple of blog posts from the Active Directory PowerShell blog explaining the advanced filters, which are as follows:

`http://blogs.msdn.com/b/adpowershell/`
`archive/2009/04/03/active-directory-powershell-`
`advanced-filter.aspx`

`http://blogs.msdn.com/b/adpowershell/`
`archive/2009/04/14/active-directory-powershell-`
`advanced-filter-part-ii.aspx`

Now that we know how to search for a single group in Active Directory, let's see how we can perform a search for multiple groups using the Get-ADGroup cmdlet.

Groups that match a particular naming convention can be queried using the following command:

```
Get-ADGroup -Filter {Name -like '*test*'}
```

This command will return all group objects that have the string test in their Name property.

The -Filter parameter can be further customized to cater to various searching needs. For example, we can extend our previous code to search for groups that contain the string Domain in their Name attribute. Look at the following command:

```
Get-ADGroup -Filter {Name -like '*test*' -or Name -like '*Domain*'}
```

Similarly, if you have a list of groups in a text file and you want to know whether they are present in Active Directory, we can use the following code:

```
$Groups = Get-Content c:\temp\Groups.txt
foreach($Group in $Groups) {
  $GroupObj = Get-ADGroup -Filter {Name -eq $Group}
  if($GroupObj) {
    "{0} : Group Found" -f $Group
  } else {
        "{0} : Group NOT Found" -f $Group
    }
}
```

This is a simple code that reads the group names from a text file located at `c:\temp\groups.txt`, loops through each group name in the text file, and checks whether it is present in Active Directory or not.

Once you have the object information of the group you are looking for, it is easy to modify the group object information using the `Set-ADGroup` cmdlet. Group object information is the display name of the group, description, group type, and so on. Modifying the membership of the groups doesn't fall within the scope of this chapter. The next chapter will talk in detail about membership modification.

The following command will help in adding a description to the group objects. The `Get-ADGroup` cmdlet will query Active Directory based on the provided filters and the results are passed to the `Set-ADGroup` cmdlet so that it can set the description to a defined string:

```
Get-ADGroup -Filter {Name -eq "TestGroup" } | Set-ADGroup -
    Description "This Group Created for testing purpose only"
```

If you want to update the description for all groups that have `Test` in their name, then the following command can be used:

```
Get-ADGroup -Filter {Name -like "*Test*" }  | Set-ADGroup -
    Description "This Group is created for testing purpose"
```

Similarly, `GroupScope` can be changed using the `Set-ADGroup` cmdlet, as shown in the following command:

```
Get-ADGroup -Filter {Name -eq "TestGroup" } | Set-ADGroup -GroupScope
    DomainLocal
```

To see the current scope, and the group category of the group, you can use the following command:

```
Get-ADGroup -Identity TestGroup | select Name, GroupCategory,
    GroupScope
```

The output will look like the following screenshot:

```
PS C:\> Get-ADGroup -Identity TestGroup | select Name, GroupCategory, GroupScope

Name                                              GroupCategory                              GroupScope
----                                              -------------                              ----------
TestGroup                                         Security                                   DomainLocal

PS C:\>
```

Also, the group type (security/distribution) can be changed by passing the required type to the `-GroupCategory` parameter of the `Set-ADGroup` cmdlet, as shown in the following command:

```
Get-ADGroup -Filter {Name -like "*Test*" }  | Set-ADGroup -
  GroupCategory Distribution
```

> Groups can be configured as e-mail-enabled security groups, which helps in both sending e-mails and granting security permissions. Since e-mail-enabled security groups require Microsoft Exchange installation, this topic is not covered here. The Microsoft Exchange PowerShell snap-in has a cmdlet that can configure a security group as a mail-enabled security group.

So far, you learned about searching for groups; now let's move forward to the important topic of group membership modification.

Adding members to a group

In the previous sections, we saw how to create groups in Active Directory, how to search for them, and how to change group object information. Groups are useless without members in them. In this section, we will concentrate on how to add both user accounts and computer accounts to security groups in Active Directory.

Like any other operation, Active Directory module has a cmdlet to add members to groups. The `Get-ADGroupMember` cmdlet does this for you.

To add a member to the group, use the `Add-ADGroupMember` cmdlet with the `member` parameter. Use the `samaccountName` of the member/user for ease of addition.

Adding user accounts to groups

Adding a single user account to a security group is very straightforward with the `Add-ADGroupMember` cmdlet, as shown in the following command:

```
Add-ADGroupMember -Identity "Group1-Read" -Members LabUser1
```

Multiple users can be added to security groups by passing their names to the `-Members` attribute as shown in the following command:

```
Add-ADGroupMember -Identity "Group1-Read" -Members
  LabUser1,LabUser2,LabUser3
```

Say you want to add a single user to multiple groups at the same time. This can be achieved by using following command:

```
"TestGroup","Group1-Read" | % {Add-ADGroupMember -Identity $_ -
   Members LabUser3 }
```

The preceding command will add the `LabUser3` user account to the `TestGroup` and `Group-Read` groups. Here, we pass group names to the `identity` parameter of the `Add-ADGroupMember` cmdlet one after the other to add `LabUser3`.

One of the common use cases for system administrators is that they will have a list of users to be added in a text file. When you have such a requirement, adding the users to a specific group is as simple as the following command:

```
$Users = Get-Content C:\temp\users.txt
```

```
Add-ADGroupMember -Identity TestGroup -Members $Users
```

In the previous example, we saw how to add user accounts to a text file. Now, let's see how to add all users from an Organizational Unit to a security group by using the following command:

```
$Users = Get-ADUser -SearchBase "OU=LAB,DC=techibee,dc=ad" -Filter
   {objectclass -eq "User" }
```

```
Add-ADGroupMember -Identity TestGroup -Members $Users
```

The first line in the preceding code will query all users in the given Organizational Unit and store the details in the `$User` variable. The same variable is passed to the `-Members` parameter of the `Add-ADGroupMember` cmdlet in the second line. This kind of additional cmdlet is useful if you have an OU structure based on departments, buildings, and offices, and you want to add all sales users to one security group, all users in the same building to another security group, and so on.

Similarly, we can copy members from one security group to another by following a sample command:

```
$members = Get-ADGroupMember -Identity TestGroup
```

```
Add-ADGroupMember -Identity TestGroup-Copy -Members $members
```

The first line reads the membership details of the `TestGroup` security group and stores it in a variable. Then, the same variable is passed to the `Add-ADGroupMember` cmdlet to add members to a new security group `TestGroup-Copy`. Here, you should note that the target group should be created beforehand.

Adding computer accounts to groups

Adding computer accounts to groups is no different than adding users. All you need to do is just replace the user name with the computer account name. The only thing that you need to do is add the suffix dollar ($) symbol to the computer name while attempting the addition.

To add a single computer account to a security group, use the following command:

```
Add-ADGroupMember -Identity TestGroup -Members "COMP1$"
```

You might wonder why the dollar sign should be used along with the computer name. This is simple. In Active Directory, each computer's SamaccountName is stored in the same format. To check SamaccountName of a computer, use the following command snippet:

```
Get-ADComputer -Identity COMP1 | select SamaccountName
```

You might wonder why we add computers to security groups. Many organizations create Group Policies and target them to list computer names by adding the computer accounts to a security group and granting apply permissions to that group alone. Similarly, such groups based on the computer accounts are used for tasks such as software deployments, performing reboots, scheduling jobs, and so on.

Computer accounts can be added to security groups based on a certain string in their name. For example, each organization will have a naming standard; for example, all test computers might have a string TEST somewhere in their name, and production could have a string such as PROD in the name. In such cases, if you would like to automatically add all TEST servers to one security group and all PROD severs to another security group, you can utilize the following sample example, adjust it according to your needs, and schedule it so that all new computers will be added to the groups automatically.

To do this, first let's read the computers with TEST in their name to a variable called $TestServers, and all computers that have PROD in their name to $ProdServers. We can do this by using the Get-ADComputer cmdlet with a filter. as shown in the following command:

```
$TestServers = Get-ADComputer -Filter {Name -like "*TEST*"}
$ProdServers = Get-ADComputer -Filter {Name -like "*PROD*" }
```

Once these variables are populated with the computer accounts, we can add them to the designated groups by using the `Add-ADGroupMember` cmdlet, as shown in the following command, by passing them to the `-Members` parameter:

```
Add-ADGroupMember -Identity "All Test Servers" -Members $TestServers
Add-ADGroupMember -Identity "All Prod Servers" -Members $ProdServers
```

After running the preceding command, all your TEST computers should be added to the `All Test Servers` security group and all the PROD servers should be added to the `All Prod Servers` security group. The membership of these groups can be viewed by the `Get-ADGroupMember` cmdlet.

So far we discussed various ways of adding members to security groups. This is not an exhaustive list and the requirement can be different from case to case. So all you need to remember is, you should have the users/computers that you want to add saved to a variable. Then, you just need to pass it to the `Add-ADGroupMember` cmdlet to add them to the required group.

Adding one group as a member to an other

In previous sections, we saw how to add user accounts and computer accounts to security groups by using the Active Directory cmdlets. Another common Active Directory operation related to security groups is adding one security group to another security group. This is done for ease of management of permissions and memberships.

Before proceeding to see how groups can be nested, let's first understand what type (scope) of groups can be added to a given security group. Without this, you might run into errors such as the following and start scratching your head to see where it went wrong:

```
PS C:\> Add-ADGroupMember -Identity "App Owners" -Members TestGroup
Add-ADGroupMember : A universal group cannot have a local group as a member
At line:1 char:1
+ Add-ADGroupMember -Identity "App Owners" -Members TestGroup
+ ~~~~~~~~~~~~~~~~~~~~~~~~~~~~~~~~~~~~~~~~~~~~~~~~~~~~~~~~~~~~~~
    + CategoryInfo          : NotSpecified: (App Owners:ADGroup) [Add-ADGroupMember], ADException
    + FullyQualifiedErrorId : ActiveDirectoryServer:8518,Microsoft.ActiveDirectory.Management.Commands.AddADGroupMembe
   r

PS C:\>
```

If you read the error message carefully, it clearly states that a universal group cannot be added to a domain local group. It is good to know these things before attempting to add a group in another group.

The TechNet article at `http://technet.microsoft.com/en-us/library/` `dn579255.aspx` gives a clear overview of different security group types, their allowed membership details, and scope conversion details. In short:

- A universal group can hold global and universal groups from any domain in the same forest as members
- A global group can hold other global groups from the same forest
- A domain local group can hold global groups from any domain (including trusted), universal groups from the same forest, domain groups from the same domain, and global and universal groups from other forests

Once you are familiar with groups, let's start with simple group nesting using the following command:

```
Add-ADGroupMember -Identity TestGroup -Members TestGroup1
```

This command adds a group named `TestGroup1` to `TestGroup`. If you notice, we are not providing any group scope information at the time of adding. The cmdlet will automatically calculate the groups and, if the addition is not supported, it will throw errors; otherwise, execution should get completed without any errors.

As you can see in the following screenshot, the group `TestGroup1` is added to `TestGroup`:

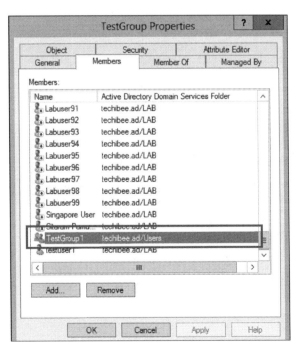

As we saw in the examples of adding bulk users and computer accounts to a group, security groups can be added in bulk as well. For this demonstration, I created 100 security groups in Active Directory so that I can add them to a new security group in bulk.

Creating bulk groups is very easy if they share a similar naming convention, as shown in the following code:

```
1..100 | % {
$GroupName = "ChildGroup{0}" -f $_
New-ADGroup -Name $GroupName -GroupScope DomainLocal -Path
   "OU=Groups,OU=PROD,DC=techibee,DC=AD"
}
```

Running the preceding code from PowerShell created 100 groups with the name `ChildGroupX` in hardly 4 to 5 seconds. Now, these can be added to another security group as a members.

First, let's create a group to which we want to add these newly created 100 groups. As we saw before, a group can be created by using the `New-ADGroup` cmdlet. The following command will create the `ParentGroup1` security group:

```
New-AdGroup -Name ParentGroup1 -GroupScope DomainLocal
```

Once the preceding group is created, we can add the newly created 100 `ChildGroup` value to the preceding group using the following command:

```
$Groups = Get-ADGroup -Filter { Name -like "ChildGroup*" }

Add-ADGroupMember -Identity ParentGroup1 -Members $Groups
```

The first line of the code will search Active Directory for any group that has a name starting with `ChildGroup` and stores the details in the `$Groups` variable. Once the details are available, they can be added to another security group, `ParentGroup1`, using the `Add-ADGroupMember` cmdlet as shown in the code on the next page.

Listing members of a security group in Active Directory

So far we saw the addition of various Active Directory objects (users, computers, and groups) to security groups, but how do we know that they are actually added? How do we find out the current members of a given security group?

These questions can be simply answered with the Get-ADGroupMember cmdlet in Active Directory. As the name of the cmdlet indicates, it queries the members of a given group. For example, let's see the membership of one of the groups that we updated in the previous example, by using the following command:

```
Get-ADGroupMember -Identity ParentGroup1 | Measure-Object
Get-ADGroupMember -Identity ParentGroup1 | select Name
```

Refer to the following screenshot of the preceding command for more clarity:

```
Administrator: Windows PowerShell

PS C:\> Get-ADGroupMember -Identity ParentGroup1 | Measure-Object


Count     : 100
Average   :
Sum       :
Maximum   :
Minimum   :
Property  :


PS C:\> Get-ADGroupMember -Identity ParentGroup1 | select Name

Name
----
ChildGroup100
ChildGroup99
ChildGroup98
ChildGroup97
ChildGroup96
ChildGroup95
```

The Measure-Object cmdlet shows how many objects are returned from the Get-ADGroupMember cmdlet when queried for the members of ParentGroup1. Remember that this is the same group where we added several child groups in the previous section while demonstrating the nested group addition operation. The second command shows the actual members. For ease of understanding, I just selected the Name property from the output using the select parameter.

As mentioned before, groups can have users, computers, and other groups as members, but how do we know the object type of each member? This can be achieved by reading the ObjectClass property of the returned objects from the Get-ADGroupMember cmdlet as shown in the following command:

```
Get-ADGroupMember -Identity TestGroup | select Name, ObjectClass
```

As you can see in the following screenshot, the `TestGroup` security group has one computer, one group, and a few users as members:

```
PS C:\> Get-ADGroupMember -Identity TestGroup | select Name, ObjectClass

Name                                                          ObjectClass
----                                                          -----------
TestGroup1                                                    group
COMP1                                                         computer
Labuser1                                                      user
DaveW                                                         user
abc                                                           user
testuser1                                                     user
admin1                                                        user


PS C:\>
```

If you are only interested in users who are part of a given group, then you can adjust the query as shown in the following command:

```
Get-ADGroupMember -Identity TestGroup | ? {$_.ObjectClass -eq "User"
   } | select Name
```

This command queries all members and returns the objects that have the object class set to `user`, which means user objects. In the same way, the filter parameter can be adjusted to return only computer accounts or groups.

If a security group holds another security group as a member, then how do we know the recursive member's details? The `Get-ADGroupMember` cmdlet has a switch parameter called `Recursive`, which can be used to query nested group memberships, as shown in the following command:

```
Get-ADGroupMember -Identity TestGroup -Recursive | select Name,
   ObjectClass
```

As you can see in the following screenshot, a new member is now a part of `TestGroup`, and `TestGroup1`, which was there earlier, does not appear in the output anymore:

```
PS C:\> Get-ADGroupMember -Identity TestGroup -Recursive | select Name, ObjectClass

Name                                                              ObjectClass
----                                                              -----------
COMP1                                                             computer
Labuser1                                                          user
DaveW                                                             user
abc                                                               user
testuser1                                                         user
admin1                                                            user
Labuser35                                                         user
Labuser34                                                         user
Labuser33                                                         user
Labuser32                                                         user
Labuser31                                                         user
Labuser30                                                         user

PS C:\>
```

Since we used the `Recursive` switch while querying, it checks for group objects in membership, queries their members, and displays the results. Even if the nested group, `TestGroup1`, has other groups in its membership, the members of that group will also be displayed when group membership is queried recursively.

Group membership of a security group can be easily exported to CSV (or Excel) using the `Export-CSV` cmdlet in PowerShell. All we need to do is just pass the output of `Get-ADGroupMember` to this cmdlet, as shown in the following command:

```
Get-ADGroupMember -Identity TestGroup | select Name,
    DistinguishedName,ObjectClass | Export-csv
    c:\temp\GroupMembership.csv -NoTypeInformation
```

In the preceding example name, DN, and the object class of `TestGroup` members are exported to a CSV file situated in the `c:\temp` folder. After export, the content of the CSV file look like the following screenshot:

	A	B	C
1	Name	DistinguishedName	ObjectClass
2	TestGroup1	CN=TestGroup1,CN=Users,DC=techibee,DC=ad	group
3	COMP1	CN=COMP1,CN=Computers,DC=techibee,DC=ad	computer
4	Labuser1	CN=Labuser1,OU=LAB,DC=techibee,DC=ad	user
5	DaveW	CN=DaveW,OU=LAB,DC=techibee,DC=ad	user
6	abc	CN=abc,OU=LAB,DC=techibee,DC=ad	user
7	testuser1	CN=testuser1,OU=LAB,DC=techibee,DC=ad	user
8	admin1	CN=admin1,OU=LAB,DC=techibee,DC=ad	user
9			

Removing members from an AD group

As part of reconciliation activities, a system administrator may need to remove members from security groups or users who have left the organization or moved to a different department and no longer require access to a particular network resource/shared drive. These changes generally involve removing user accounts from a given security group.

The Active Directory PowerShell module provides a cmdlet called `Remove-ADGroupMember`. Similar to the `Get-ADGroupMember` cmdlet, the `Remove-ADGroupMember` cmdlet also has two mandatory parameters: `Identity` and `Members`. The `Identity` parameter takes the name of the group from which you want to remove the members and the `Members` parameter takes the list of users, computers, or group accounts that you want to remove.

The following sample command is used to remove a user account from a security group:

```
Remove-ADGroupMember -Identity TestGroup -Members LabUser1
```

As you can see in the following screenshot, the `Remove-ADGroupMember` cmdlet prompts for confirmation while removing an object from membership. This is just a safety measure to make the system administrator verify his action and proceed with it:

If you are sure about the action you are performing or you don't want to receive this confirmation prompt, just pass the `$false` to the `-Confirm` parameter as shown in the following command:

```
Remove-ADGroupMember -Identity TestGroup -Members LabUser1 -
  Confirm:$false
```

This won't prompt for any confirmation and just proceeds with the operation. In the preceding example, we removed a user object from the security group. To remove a computer account from the security group, you can follow a similar approach and pass the name of the computer account to the `-Members` parameter. You should remember to suffix the computer name with the dollar sign ($) just as we did for the `Add-ADGroupMember` cmdlet; otherwise, your removal will fail. The following command removes the `COMP1$` computer account from the security group:

```
Remove-ADGroupMember -Identity TestGroup -Members COMP1$ -
   Confirm:$false
```

Removing a single user or computer account from a security group is easy, but how do we perform this operation in bulk? Let's take a small example where you have a list of user or computer names in the CSV file along with the group names from which they should be removed. Now our task is to read the details from the CSV file and remove the members accordingly. A sample CSV file looks like the following screenshot. The object name is the name of the user or computer or group that you want to remove. The object type represents what type of object you want to remove and the third column holds the group name from which you want to remove the object.

	A	B	C
1	ObjectName	ObjectType	GroupName
2	COMP1	Computer	TestGroup
3	LabUser11	User	TestGroup
4	SRVMEM1	Computer	TestGroup1
5	TestGroup1	Group	TestGroup
6	LabUser12	User	TestGroup
7			

The following code processes the CSV file and performs the operations:

```
#Import the CSV file into a variable
$Removals = Import-CSV C:\temp\GroupRemovals.csv
#Loop through each entry in CSV file
foreach($entry in $Removals) {
    #Read the group Name
    $GroupName = $entry.GroupName
    #if Object type is Computer, then suffix it with $ sign
    if($entry.ObjectType -eq "Computer") {
        $AccountToRemove = "{0}`$" -f $entry.ObjectName
    } else {
        $AccountToRemove = $entry.ObjectName
    }
```

```
Write-Host "Removing a $($entry.ObjectType) account with name
    $AccountToRemove from $GroupName"
#Remove the account from Group
Remove-ADGroupMember -Identity $GroupName -Members
    $AccountToRemove -Confirm:$false
}
```

Save the preceding code in a PS1 file and run it from PowerShell. You will see an output similar to this. To run a PS1 file from PowerShell, you can give the full path of the script as shown in the following screenshot or change to the folder where you stored the PS1 file and then call it by prefixing with \ (for example, \ProcessRemovals.ps1).

```
PS C:\> C:\temp\ProcessRemovals.ps1
Removing a Computer account with name COMP1$ from TestGroup
Removing a User account with name LabUser11 from TestGroup
Removing a Computer account with name SRVMEM1$ from TestGroup1
Removing a Group account with name TestGroup1 from TestGroup
Removing a User account with name LabUser12 from TestGroup
PS C:\>
```

You can refer to the TechNet page at http://technet. microsoft.com/en-us/library/bb613481%28v=vs.85%29. aspx to understand more about how to run PS1 scripts from the PowerShell window.

The action showed in the output is self-explanatory. The code provided is also supported with sufficient comments to understand what each statement is doing. All it does is read the CSV file and store the data in an array. The code then loops through each item in the array and processes the removal operations. If the entry has a computer object, then it suffixes the dollar sign to the computer name so that it completes the execution without any error.

Deleting a security group

When a group is no longer required, it needs to be removed or deleted from Active Directory in order to keep the database clean and up-to-date. Before performing the delete operation, make sure it has no members inside it. If there are members and this group is provisioned for any network resources access, then the user will face problems. Once the group is deleted, it is difficult to revert the change unless you have efficient restoration mechanisms in your environment. Also, performing such restore operations is not straightforward and can be done only by specialists. Given these reasons, it is important to ensure that there are no members in the group before deletion.

A security group in Active Directory can be deleted using the `Remove-ADGroup` cmdlet. Similar to removing group membership, deleting the group also prompts for confirmation. It can be suppressed by using the same logic that we applied while dealing with the `Remove-ADGroupMember` cmdlet, as shown in the following command:

```
Remove-ADGroup -Identity TestGroup1 -Confirm:$false
```

Groups that need to be deleted can be searched using the `Get-ADGroup` cmdlet and the output can be passed to the `Remove-ADGroup` cmdlet for deletion, as shown in the following command:

```
Get-ADGroup -Filter "Name -like 'TestGroup*'" | Remove-ADGroup -
   Confirm:$false
```

As shown in the following screenshot, `Get-ADGroup` returned a few groups when we searched for groups starting with the string `TestGroup`:

```
PS C:\> Get-ADGroup -Filter "Name -like 'TestGroup*'" | select Name

Name
----
TestGroup
TestGroup-Copy
TestGroup1
TestGroup1
TestGroup2

PS C:\> Get-ADGroup -Filter "Name -like 'TestGroup*'" | Remove-ADGroup -Confirm:$false
PS C:\>
```

All these groups are passed to `Remove-ADGroup` via a pipeline and with the `-Confirm` option set to `$false`. This will delete all the security groups that have names starting with `TestGroup`.

Summary

Throughout this chapter, we saw various operations related to group membership changes such as the addition and removal of Active Directory objects, which include users, computers, and groups from security groups. The group management using PowerShell resolves mostly around a handful of cmdlets such as `Get-ADGroup`, `Add-ADGroupMember`, `Remove-ADGroupMember`, `Set-ADGroup`, and `Remove-ADGroup`. Getting familiar with these cmdlets helps you perform group modifications very easily.

In the next chapter, we will see how to manage Group Policies using PowerShell. This is another important topic every system administrator should learn because troubleshooting Group Policies is a daily job, and one should know how PowerShell helps in simplifying these tasks.

4
Configuring Group Policies

We saw user, computer, and group object management in the previous chapters. This chapter will take you through **Group Policy Objects (GPO)** management in Active Directory. Group Policies are widely used in the Windows environment for several purposes. Several user and computer settings can be managed and controlled in the Windows domain environment using PowerShell.

In this chapter, we will cover the following topics:

- Installing Group Policies
- Querying Group Polices
- Creating and linking Group Policies
- Working with Group Policy permissions
- Generating Resultant Set Of Policies
- Removing Group Policy links and objects

We will explore various Group Policy operations such as creation, modification, linking, enforcing, and searching for GPOs using PowerShell. Group Policies in the Microsoft environment can be easily managed using Group Policy PowerShell module. This module is available by default when a Windows Server 2008 R2 or later operating system is promoted to domain controller. This module can be installed on a Windows Server 2008 R2 or on later member servers by installing **GPMC (Group Policy Management Console)**. This module can be made available on client operating systems such as Windows 7 or later by installing **Remove Server Administration Tools (RSAT)**. It contains the GPMC installation, which in turn will provide the Group Policy module.

Installing the Group Policy module

Let's see how to install the GPMC console in Windows Server 2008 R2, which includes the Group Policy PowerShell module as well.

Like any other Windows feature, **Group Policy Management** can be installed from Server Manager using the **Add Features Wizard**. Select the **Group Policy Management** option, as shown in the following screenshot, to install the **Group Policy Management** console as well as the Group Policy PowerShell module. Select the aforementioned option and click **Next** in the wizard to complete the installation.

Similarly, the console can be installed on Windows Server 2012 R2 and it works in a similar way. From Server Manager, you need to add the **Group Policy Management** option to install this feature as shown in the following screenshot:

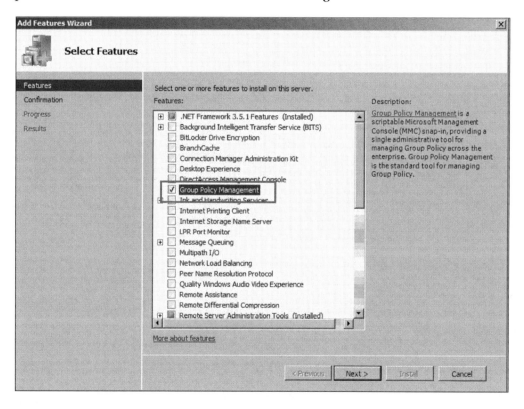

Group Policy Management feature can be installed using PowerShell as well. To check the current status of this feature installation, try the following command in the PowerShell window:

```
Get-WindowsFeature -Name GPMC
```

As highlighted in the following screenshot, the cross mark under the **Display Name** field indicates that the GPMC windows feature is installed. The **Install State** column indicates the installation status:

```
PS C:\> Get-WindowsFeature -Name GPMC

Display Name                                          Name              Install State
------------                                          ----              -------------
[X] Group Policy Management                           GPMC                  Installed

PS C:\>
```

If you find that the GPMC feature is not installed, then it can be installed using the `Add-WindowsFeature` cmdlet in Server Manager module. This cmdlet takes the name of the feature to be installed. Passing the value GPMC to the `Name` parameter will install the GPMC feature automatically.

> The `Get-WindowsFeature` cmdlet is part of the Server Manager module. This module gets imported automatically when you call this cmdlet in Windows Server 2012 or later. However, in Windows Server 2008 R2, you need to explicitly import the Server Manager module using the `Import-Module` cmdlet to use `Get-WindowsFeature`. Another thing to note is you might not see the **Install State** column when you execute `Get-WindowsFeature` in Windows Server 2008 R2.

The installation takes a few minutes and the progress bar shows the progress. Once the module is installed, you can start using it by importing the following command:

```
Import-Module GroupPolicy
```

You can view the list of cmdlets inside this module using the following command:

```
Get-Command -Module GroupPolicy
```

Running this code lists all the cmdlets available in the module. There are in all 28 cmdlets in this module; they can help us to perform various Group Policy-related operations. The following table contains some of the frequently used cmdlets in the Group Policy module; we will use them in further sections of this chapter:

Cmdlet Name	Description
New-GPO	Creates a new Group Policy Object (GPO)
New-GPLink	Links an existing GPO to a site, domain, or OU
Remove-GPO	Deletes/Removes a GPO

Cmdlet Name	Description
Remove-GPLink	Unlinks a GPO from a site, domain, or OU.
Invoke-GPUpdate	This is available only in Windows 2012, Windows 8, or later versions. Used to refresh Group Policy settings on remote computers by scheduling and running the GPUpdate.exe command on the computer.
Get-GPO	Fetches GP object information for the specified name.
Get-GPOReport	Generates reports in XML or HTML format for a specified GPO.
Get-GPPermission(s)	The command is just a permission in Windows 2012 and permissions in Windows 2008 R2. Gets permission levels for one or more security principals for a specified GPO.
Set-GPLink	Used to set properties such as Enabled/Enforced/Order for a specified GPO link.

Querying Group Policies

Active Directory in large environments contains policies ranging from a few tens to hundreds in number, based on need and usage criteria. These policies will be linked to multiple places in the Active Directory structure such as domains, OUs, and sites. The Get-GPO cmdlet in the Group Policy module helps in querying the details of Group Policies at various levels.

To see all Group Policies in the current forest, you can use the following command:

```
Get-GPO -All
```

By default, all the Group Policy cmdlets contact the **Primary Domain Controller** (**PDC**) emulator to get these results. If you want to query the details from the local domain controller, you can pass the name of the domain controller with the -Server parameter, using the following command:

```
Get-GPO -All -Server TIBDC2
```

Here, TIBDC2 is a domain controller in a local LAN. The output returned by this code contains name, **Global Unique Identifier** (**GUID**), Creation-Time, Modification-Time, and other details.

If you want to see all the Group Policies modified in the last 24 hours, you can use the following command:

```
$datetime = (Get-Date).AddHours(-24)
Get-GPO -All | ? {$_.Modificationtime -gt $datetime }
```

First, we will store the details of the last 24 hours in the $datetime variable by passing the -24 value to the AddHours method of Get-Date. So, the $datetime variable will contain the date and time details of the previous day. Later, we will be comparing the Modification-Time of each GPO to see if it is modified after the stored date. Look at the following screenshot for the sample output. If no GPOs are modified in the last 24 hours, you will not see any results:

```
PS C:\> $datetime = (Get-Date).AddHours(-24)
PS C:\> $datetime

Wednesday, 15 October 2014 11:51:03 PM


PS C:\> Get-GPO -All | ? {$_.Modificationtime -gt $datetime }


DisplayName      : LogonPolicy
DomainName       : techibee.ad
Owner            : techibee\Domain Admins
Id               : 98cbbc75-de94-4093-9b46-d4100230849e
GpoStatus        : AllSettingsEnabled
Description      :
CreationTime     : 19/6/2014 2:52:01 PM
ModificationTime : 16/10/2014 11:50:00 PM
UserVersion      : AD Version: 2, SysVol Version: 2
ComputerVersion  : AD Version: 0, SysVol Version: 0
WmiFilter        :
```

Similarly, if you want to list all the Group Policies linked to the given Organizational Unit, the Get-GPO cmdlet can be used in following manner:

```
Import-Module ActiveDirectory
$LinkedGPOs = Get-ADOrganizationalUnit -Filter 'Name -like
    "*lab*"' | select -ExpandProperty LinkedGroupPolicyObjects
$GUIDRegex = "{[a-zA-Z0-9]{8}[-][a-zA-Z0-9]{4}[-][a-zA-Z0-9]{4}[-
    ][a-zA-Z0-9]{4}[-][a-zA-Z0-9]{12}}"

foreach($LinkedGPO in $LinkedGPOs) {
    $result = [Regex]::Match($LinkedGPO,$GUIDRegex);
    if($result.Success) {
        $GPOGuid = $result.Value.TrimStart("{").TrimEnd("}")
        Get-GPO -Guid $GPOGuid
    }
}
```

For the preceding code, refer to the following steps:

1. In the preceding code, first we query the object of the given Organizational Unit, with the name lab by the Get-ADOrganizationalUnit cmdlet and storing the value of the LinkedGroupPolicyObjects property into the $LinkedGPOs variable.

2. You need to import the Active Directory module to make use of the `Get-ADOrganizationalUnit` cmdlet. The output returned by this cmdlet in the preceding code is an array of items that contains the details of Group Policies linked to the given OU. The details returned by the cmdlet contain the value of the `gpLink` attribute, if you check the properties of LAB OU using `Adsiedit.msc`.

3. Using a for loop, we loop through each link and extract the GUID of Group Policy into a variable after trimming out the curly braces. Trimming the braces is necessary as the `Get-GPO` cmdlet needs GUID without braces.

4. Then pass the GUID to the `Get-GPO` cmdlet to get the details of the GPO.

You can also save the preceding code into a PS1 file and run it from the PowerShell window. Remember the procedure for running PS1 files from a PowerShell window; it will show the details of the Group Policies that are currently linked. As you can see in the following screenshot, the LAB OU has two Group Policies linked to it and this output matches the details that GPMC shows:

```
PS C:\> C:\temp\Get-GPsLinkedToOU.ps1


DisplayName       : LogonPolicy
DomainName        : techibee.ad
Owner             : techibee\Domain Admins
Id                : 98cbbc75-de94-4093-9b46-d4100230849e
GpoStatus         : AllSettingsEnabled
Description       :
CreationTime      : 19/6/2014 2:52:01 PM
ModificationTime  : 16/10/2014 11:50:00 PM
UserVersion       : AD Version: 2, SysVol Version: 2
ComputerVersion   : AD Version: 0, SysVol Version: 0
WmiFilter         :

DisplayName       : ComputerPolicy
DomainName        : techibee.ad
Owner             : techibee\Domain Admins
Id                : db5f0bd6-b114-4850-aeb0-88f10d3158de
GpoStatus         : AllSettingsEnabled
Description       :
CreationTime      : 28/7/2014 11:49:36 AM
ModificationTime  : 28/7/2014 11:49:36 AM
UserVersion       : AD Version: 0, SysVol Version: 0
ComputerVersion   : AD Version: 0, SysVol Version: 0
WmiFilter         :


PS C:\>
```

Refer to the following screenshot to understand this better:

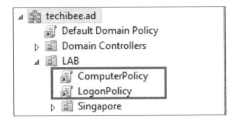

Similarly, you can find Group Policies linked to any OU by just changing the filter in the code. For example, you can query the GPOs linked to PROD OU by changing the filter value of `Get-ADOrganizationalUnit` in the previous code, as shown in the following command:

```
$LinkedGPOs = Get-ADOrganizationalUnit -Filter 'Name -like "PROD"' |
   select -ExpandProperty LinkedGroupPolicyObjects
```

Group Policies can be linked to the domain level as well as the site level. To view the Group Policies linked to the domain level, parse the value of the `LinkedGroupPolicyObjects` property returned by the `Get-ADDomain` cmdlet. The following command helps you to fetch the GPOs linked to domain level:

```
Get-ADDomain   | select LinkedGroupPolicyObjects
```

More about the format in which GPO details are stored in the `gpLink` attribute is available at `http://msdn.microsoft.com/en-us/library/cc232505.aspx`.

Creating and linking Group Policies

So far, we have seen how to query the existing Group Policies using the Active Directory and Group Policy modules. Now, let's check how to create a new policy in Active Directory and link it to Organizational Units using PowerShell code.

To do this, we mainly need two cmdlets:

- `New-GPO`: This will help in creating the Group Policies
- `New-GPLink`: This will help in creating links to existing OUs, domains, and sites

To create a new GPO, we just need to pass the name of the GPO to the `New-GPO` cmdlet and it returns the GPO object details after creating the new GPO. The following command creates a new GPO with the name `MyNewGPO`:

```
New-GPO -Name "MyNewGPO"
```

It should look like following screenshot:

```
PS C:\> New-GPO -Name "MyNewGPO"

DisplayName       : MyNewGPO
DomainName        : techibee.ad
Owner             : techibee\Domain Admins
Id                : 2231a3a3-a4c9-4b93-aa08-901d2ef8ca48
GpoStatus         : AllSettingsEnabled
Description       :
CreationTime      : 17/10/2014 12:35:25 AM
ModificationTime  : 17/10/2014 12:35:25 AM
UserVersion       : AD Version: 0, SysVol Version: 0
ComputerVersion   : AD Version: 0, SysVol Version: 0
WmiFilter         :

PS C:\>
```

When a new GPO is created, it does not get linked to any OUs or domains by default. It just stays in the Group Policy objects container in the GPMC console. After creating the GPO, it has to be linked to any of the existing OUs and this can be done by using the New-GPLink cmdlet, as shown in the following command:

```
New-GPLink -Name "MyNewGPO" -Target "OU=PROD,DC=techibee,DC=AD"
```

When the preceding code is executed, it returns the results that contain details about link enable status, the order number of the GPO, enforcement status, and so on, as shown in the following screenshot:

```
PS C:\> New-GPLink -Name "MyNewGPO" -Target "OU=PROD,DC=techibee,DC=AD"

GpoId        : 2231a3a3-a4c9-4b93-aa08-901d2ef8ca48
DisplayName  : MyNewGPO
Enabled      : True
Enforced     : False
Target       : OU=Prod,DC=techibee,DC=ad
Order        : 2

PS C:\>
```

By default, the GPO link is enabled during the link creation process. If you want the link to be disabled, then pass a value No to the -LinkEnabled parameter of the New-GPLink cmdlet during the creation process. Similarly, you can control the enforcement status by the -Enforced parameter and the order of the GPO by the -Order parameter.

The following command creates a new GPO link at groups OU with default link status disabled and enforcement enabled:

```
New-GPLink -Name "MyNewGPO" -Target
  "OU=Groups,OU=PROD,DC=techibee,DC=AD" -LinkEnabled No -Enforced yes
```

After running this command, you can verify the result using the GPMC console, which shows that the newly linked policy at groups OU will have the link disabled and **Enforced** is set to **Yes**. Look at the following screenshot to understand this better:

Groups					
Linked Group Policy Objects	Group Policy Inheritance	Delegation			
Link Order	GPO		Enforced	Link Enabled	GPO Status
1	MyNewGPO		Yes	No	Enabled

From Windows Server 2008 onwards Microsoft has introduced a new concept in Group Policies, which is starter Group Policies. Starter Group Policy is like a template where you preconfigure certain settings and values. Any new Group Policy created from this starter GPO will contain the pre-defined settings in the starter GPO. Starter GPOs in Active Directory can be created using the New-GPStarterGPO cmdlet as shown in the following command:

```
New-GPStarterGPO -Name "TIB-StarterGPO"
```

After the creation of the starter GPO, add some settings to it and save it. These settings can be something you want by default whenever you create a new GPO. Once the starter GPO is created and saved, you can use it as a template and create new GPOs from the starter GPO. The new GPOs will contain the default settings you already configured in the starter GPO. Please refer to the TechNet page at http://technet.microsoft.com/en-us/library/cc753200.aspx to understand starter GPOs better.

The following command shows how to create a new GPO from an existing starter GPO:

```
New-GPO -Name "First GPO" -StarterGpoName "TIB-StarterGPO
```

In the next sections, we will see how to modify existing GPOs and GPO link objects.

Working with links, enforcements, and order of GPOs

While learning about searching for Group Policies in previous sections, you have seen how to query GPOs linked to a given OU. When a GPO is linked to an OU, **Link Enable** is set to NO and **Enforced** is also set to NO. These are defaults; however, it is possible that some of the users might change these values over a period of time based on their needs. For example, the link might be enabled, enforcement might be enabled, and many more functions similar to this. So, how do we find these details using PowerShell so that we can find the exact status of Group Policies linked to an OU? The following function will help in finding this information.

This function queries the specified OU for a list of GPOs linked, their **Link Enable** status, enforcement status, and the link order of GPOs. You can refer to the TechNet page at http://technet.microsoft.com/en-us/library/hh147307%28v=ws.10%29.aspx to understand these GPO parameters better:

```
function Get-GPOLinkStatus {
[cmdletbinding()]
param(
   [string]$OUName
)
$OUs = @(Get-ADOrganizationalUnit -Filter * -Properties gPlink | ?
   {$_.Name -eq "$OUName"})
#Return if no OUs found with given name
if(!$OUs) { Write-Warning "No such OU found"; return }

foreach($OU in $OUs) {
 $OUName = $OU.Name
 $OUDN = $OU.DistinguishedName
 #Hackey way to get LDAP strings. Regex might be best option here
 $OUGPLinks = $OU.gPlink.split("][")
 #Get rid of all empty entries the array
 $OUGPLinks =  @($OUGPLinks | ? {$_})
 $order = $OUGPLinks.count;
 foreach($GpLink in $OUGPLinks) {
  $GpName = [adsi]$GPlink.split(";")[0] | select -ExpandProperty
  displayName
  $GpStatus = $GPlink.split(";")[1]
  $EnableStatus = $EnforceStatus = 0
  switch($GPStatus) {
     "1" {$EnableStatus = $false; $EnforceStatus = $false}
     "2" {$EnableStatus = $true; $EnforceStatus = $true}
```

```
      "3" {$EnableStatus = $false; $EnforceStatus = $true}
      "0" {$EnableStatus = $true; $EnforceStatus = $false}
    }
    $OutputObj = New-Object -TypeName PSobject
    $OutputObj | Add-Member -MemberType NoteProperty -Name OUName -
    Value $OUName
    $OutputObj | Add-Member -MemberType NoteProperty -Name OUDN -
    Value $OUDN
    $OutputObj | Add-Member -MemberType NoteProperty -Name GPName -
    Value $GPName
    $OutputObj | Add-Member -MemberType NoteProperty -Name IsLinked
    -Value $EnableStatus
    $OutputObj | Add-Member -MemberType NoteProperty -Name
    IsEnforced -Value $EnforceStatus
    $OutputObj | Add-Member -MemberType NoteProperty -Name GPOrder
    -Value $Order
     $OutputObj
     $order--
   }
  }
 }
```

Copy and paste this code into the PowerShell window where you have imported the Active Directory as well as Group Policy modules, and then query the status of GPOs linked to an OU, using the following command:

```
Get-GPOLinkStatus -OUName LAB | ft -AutoSize
```

This command will query the GPO link status at the LAB OU and return the details. As you can see in the following screenshot, the LogonPolicy of the **IsLink** column is enabled, and **IsEnforced** is set to False and has the order 2. The Get-GPOLinkStatus command we used here is nothing but the function we copied to a PowerShell window in the previous section, as shown in the following screenshot:

```
PS C:\> Get-GPOLinkStatus -OUName LAB | ft -AutoSize

OUName OUDN                      GPName          IsLinked IsEnforced GPOrder
------ ----                      ------          -------- ---------- -------
LAB    OU=LAB,DC=techibee,DC=ad LogonPolicy     True     False      2
LAB    OU=LAB,DC=techibee,DC=ad ComputerPolicy  True     False      1


PS C:\>
```

This output is the same as what you see in the GPMC console. In the following screenshot, you can notice that both the Group Policies have **Link Enabled** set to **Yes** and **Enforced** set to **No**. Also, the **Link Order** column you see in GPMC matches the GPO order shown in the preceding output screenshot.

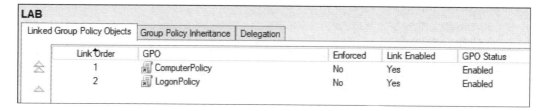

Once we know the link status, we might want to alter some information. For example, if we want to disable the link of `LogonPolicy` at LAB OU, the following command can be used:

```
Set-GPLink -Name "LogonPolicy" -Target "OU=LAB,DC=techibee,DC=AD" -
    LinkEnabled No
```

This sets the **Link Enable** status to **No** for `LogonPolicy` GPO at LAB OU.

Similarly, enforcement of a policy can be changed using the following command:

```
Set-GPLink -Name "LogonPolicy" -Target "OU=LAB,DC=techibee,DC=AD"
    Enforced yes
```

Changing the order of the policy works in a similar way, as shown by the following command:

```
Set-GPLink -Name "LogonPolicy" -Target "OU=LAB,DC=techibee,DC=AD" -
    Order 1
```

After the making the preceding changes, now the GPO's link status at LAB OU looks like the following screenshot. You can clearly notice that the LogonPolicy of the **IsLink** column is disabled, **IsEnforced** is enabled and the order changed to 1 in the following screenshot:

```
PS C:\> Get-GPOLinkStatus -OUName LAB | ft -AutoSize

OUName OUDN                          GPName         IsLinked IsEnforced GPOrder
------ ----                          ------         -------- ---------- -------
LAB    OU=LAB,DC=techibee,DC=ad ComputerPolicy     True     False          2
LAB    OU=LAB,DC=techibee,DC=ad LogonPolicy        False    True           1


PS C:\> |
```

In a similar way, the GPO's link status at domain level and site level can be changed using the `Set-GPLink` cmdlet. The only thing you need to do is just pass the DN of the domain or site to the `-Target` parameter.

Working with Group Policy permissions

System administrators often need to work with Group Policy permissions. Sometimes, we modify Group Policy permissions to deploy the GPO settings to new users/computers/groups. Similarly, we modify permissions to allow other teams to manage the Group Policy. These operations are easy if you are granting permissions to one or two users on a single GPO; however, as the volume increases, it is difficult to perform this manually and automation makes things easy in this case.

The Group Policy module has two cmdlets that can ease Group Policy permission management. They are as follows:

- `Get-GPPermission`: This is used to query the permissions that are set on a GPO
- `Set-GPPermission`: This is used to apply a new set of permissions or modify existing permissions on a GPO

If you are trying to query GPO permissions from a Windows Server 2008 or later, use the `Get-GPPermissions` and `Set-GPPermissions` cmdlets. Notice the additional 's' at the end of these cmdlets. In Windows Server 2012 and later, the `Get-GPPermissions` and `Set-GPPermissions` commands will work but they are aliases to the `Get-GPPermission` and `Set-GPPermission` cmdlets. Hence, the cmdlet names are used in this section instead of aliases. Microsoft has removed the letter "s" from both the cmdlets in Windows Server 2012 because they are not in compliance with cmdlet naming conventions. You might want to refer to the MSDN page at `http://msdn.microsoft.com/en-us/library/dd878270%28v=vs.85%29.aspx` for cmdlet naming guidelines.

Querying GPO permissions

This section will help you to understand how to query Group Policy permissions using the `Get-GPPermission` cmdlet. We need to pass either the name or GUID of the GPO for which we want to query permissions. Also, we need to specify a target object name when we want to verify what kind of permissions it has on the GPO. If you don't know the target name, then you can use the `-All` parameter to return all the permissions on the given GPO. Note that, without the `-All` or `-TargetName` and `-TargetType` parameter, the cmdlet will result in failures.

We can get the current permissions of a given GPO using the following command. As you can notice, we are using an -All parameter to retrieve the complete permissions list of this GPO:

```
Get-GPPermission -Name "MyNewGPO" -All
```

This command lists all permissions configured on MyNewGPO. However, if you are interested in permissions that domain administrators have, you can alter the query. As you can see, we have passed domain admins to the TargetName parameter and we have specified that the target we provided is a group by passing it to TargetType using the following command:

```
Get-GPPermission -Name "MyNewGPO" -TargetName "Domain Admins" -
   TargetType Group
```

Similarly, you can query the permissions assigned to any user or computer by specifying the name of the user or computer account with the TargetName parameter and by passing object type to the TargetType parameter.

Look at the following example command, where we are fetching the permissions assigned to the LabUser1 user account on MyNewGPO:

```
Get-GPPermission -Name MyNewGPO -TargetName LabUser1 -TargetType User
```

These permissions can be exported to Excel as well in CSV format using the following command:

```
Get-GPPermission -Name "MyNewGPO" -All  | export-csv
   c:\temp\MyNewGPO-Perms.csv -NoTypeInformation
```

Modifying GPO permissions

To modify the GPO permission, we can use the Set-GPPermission cmdlet. It requires the TargetName and TargetType parameter to be added as the parameters to process permissions. Along with these, we also need to provide the -PermissionLevel parameter. The valid permission levels are: GpoRead, GpoApply, GpoEdit, GpoEditDeleteModifySecurity, or None. The valid GPO permission levels are as follows:

- To grant a group GPO read permissions, we can use the following command:

    ```
    Set-GPPermission -Name "MyNewGPO" -TargetName TestGroup -
       TargetType Group -PermissionLevel GpoRead
    ```

- If you change your mind and want to adjust the permissions to `GPOApply` instead of `GPORead`, you can do this using the `-Replace` switch, with the help of the following command:

```
Set-GPPermission -Name "MyNewGPO" -TargetName TestGroup -
    TargetType Group -PermissionLevel GpoApply -Replace
```

- You can verify the status of execution by running `Get-GPPermission` using the following command:

```
Get-GPPermission -Name "MyNewGPO" -TargetName "TestGroup" -
    TargetType Group
```

As you can see in the following screenshot, `TestGroup` has `GpoApply` permission on **MyNewGPO** object:

```
PS C:\> Get-GPPermission -Name "MyNewGPO" -TargetName "TestGroup" -TargetType Group


Trustee      : TestGroup
TrusteeType  : Alias
Permission   : GpoApply
Inherited    : False


PS C:\>
```

Similarly, if you want to remove permission for `TestGroup` on the GPO, then just change the `-PermissionLevel` parameter to `None` as shown by the following command:

```
Set-GPPermission -Name "MyNewGPO" -TargetName TestGroup -TargetType
    Group -PermissionLevel None
```

You can use a similar approach to grant permissions to users or computer accounts on a GPO by changing `-TargetType` to user or computer.

Updating Group Policy and generating Resultant Set of Policy

So far, we have seen operations related to Group Policy objects such as creation and modifications. Now, let's see how to apply these GPOs and find out the Group Policy's update status.

Remotely triggering Group Policy update

Group Policy update on a system can be triggered on a computer using the gpupdate.exe utility. The Invoke-GPUpdate cmdlet in the Group Policy module functions the same way and also allows triggering of GP update on computers remotely. This cmdlet can be used to trigger computer or user policy update selectively and also provides options to control, reboot, or logoff after the GPO process.

> Note: The Invoke-GPUpdate cmdlet is available on Windows Server 2012/Windows 8 and later only. However, you can use this cmdlet from Windows Server 2012/Windows 8 or later to trigger Group Policy update on Windows Server 2008, Windows Server 2008 R2, and Windows 7.

The following command can trigger synchronous Group Policy update on TIB-WIN8PC remotely:

```
Invoke-GPUpdate -Computer TIB-WIN8PC -Sync
```

By default, the preceding command will not cause reboot or logoff of the remote computer unless you specify either one of the -Boot or -Logoff switches, as shown by the following command:

```
Invoke-GPUpdate -Computer TIB-WIN8PC -Sync -Boot -Target Computer
```

This command triggers the computer Group Policy update and forces a reboot after processing, if any of the GPO **Client Side Extensions** (**CSE**) requires a reboot to complete the GPO processing.

Similarly, logoff can be allowed with the -Logoff switch using the following command:

```
Invoke-GPUpdate -Computer TIB-WIN8PC -Sync -Target user -LogOff
```

If you have a list of computers where you want to trigger GP update, you can use the following command:

```
Get-Content c:\temp\comps.txt | % { Invoke-GPUpdate -Computer $_ -Sync }
```

Also, if you want to trigger GP update on all computers in an OU, you can do this using the following command:

```
Get-ADComputer -Filter * -SearchBase "OU=LAB,DC=techibee,dc=ad" | % {
    Invoke-GPUpdate -Computer $_.Name -Sync }
```

This queries all computers in LAB OU and triggers GP updates on them.

Collecting RSOP data remotely

Resultant Set Of Policies (RSOP) output shows which policies are applied for a user or computer, if any policies are denied or not applied, what is the reason for it, when the policies are applied, and other details.

The `Get-GPResultantSetOfPolicy` cmdlet helps to find this information. It queries remote computer for RSOP data and generates a report in HTML or XML format. By default, it queries the computer's RSOP information; if a user account's RSOP information is needed then the name of the user should be passed to the `-User` parameter as shown in the following command:

```
Get-GPResultantSetOfPolicy -Computer TIB-Win8PC -ReportType HTML -
   Path c:\temp\TIB-WIN8PCReport.html
```

To include a user account's RSOP data in the output, add the `-user` parameter and pass the name of the user as shown in the following command:

```
Get-GPResultantSetOfPolicy -Computer TIB-Win8PC -ReportType HTML -
   Path c:\temp\TIB-WIN8PCReport.html -User techibee.ad\testuser1
```

These commands save the RSOP results in HTML format in the `c:\temp` folder with the given name. This HTML will contain information related to a list of applicable GPOs, their apply status, any errors that occurred during the GPO processing, and so on.

The XML report type is useful when you want to collect the RSOP data and process it further programmatically to find certain information. For general analysis, the HTML format is sufficient and is much more readable.

Removing Group Policy links and objects

It is good to remove Group Policy objects and their links when they are no longer in use. Otherwise, it will create additional confusion while reviewing the policies through GPMC UI tools and also analyzing the GP result output from such environments is time-consuming as the computers and users have to process policies that are just linked to an OU but doesn't apply any policy to an object in particular.

The Group Policy module provides two cmdlets for this cleanup work, namely `Remove-GPO` and `Remove-GPLink`. As their names indicate, their purpose is to remove Group Policy and its links from an OU, domain, or site as shown by the following command:

```
Remove-GPO LogonPolicy
```

This command deletes the `LogonPolicy` GPO from the Group Policies store and also deletes links from OUs where it was linked. Use this approach when you are completely retiring the particular GPO from your environment. Removing a GPO causes its data to get deleted from the **SYSVOL** share folder and related objects in Active Directory will get deleted as well. So, be sure to choose this option as the restoration of GPOs is not straightforward like other Active Directory objects.

Say, for example, you want to delete the link of a GPO from a particular OU but not the GPO itself, then you can use the `Remove-GPLink` cmdlet, as shown in the following command:

```
Remove-GPLink -Name MyNewGPO -Target "OU=PROD,DC=techibee,DC=ad"
```

The preceding command unlinks the `MyNewGPO` from PROD OU. You can read more details about these cmdlets by querying their help content using the `Get-Help` cmdlet.

Summary

In this chapter, you have learned about a new module, Group Policy, and how to use it to perform some of the GPO related operations. We covered topics starting from creation of GPOs, modifying them, linking them, working with other options such as enforcement, working with permissions for the removal of GPOs and their links.

We also covered RSOP generation, which is a very common and frequent task for any level of system administrator; using automation in this area saves time significantly as the operations can be done remotely without interacting with the end user.

In the next chapter, we will look into management of Organizational Units, domains, trusts, and sites with PowerShell in detail. There, you will understand how to create OUs, sites, and subnets. You will also learn about how to query domain details and domain controller details of a domain or forest.

5
Managing Domains, Organizational Units, Sites, and Subnets

We have discussed about managing various Active Directory objects (such as users, computers, groups, and so on.) using PowerShell in previous chapters. Active Directory administration will not end with managing just users and computers. As an Active Directory administrator, one needs to manage several core components of Active Directory such as domains, trusts, sites, subnets, Organizational Units, and so on.

In this chapter, we will focus on the following:

- Querying forest and domain details
- Managing Organizational Units
- Working with sites and subnets

Managing domains

Most small organizations comprise only one domain in their environment where all users, computers, and other resources are created and managed. These are called **single-forest**, **single-domain** environments. However, in large scale organizations, there might be a complex environment containing several forests, each forest containing several domains with different types of trusts across domains and forests. In this section, you will learn to query these details using PowerShell.

Active Directory module has several cmdlets that can help in querying the forest and domain details. To get the list of cmdlets that work with a domain or forest, run the following commands after importing the Active Directory module:

```
Get-Command -Module ActiveDirectory -Name *Domain*
Get-Command -Module ActiveDirectory -Name *Forest*
```

Each of the previous commands will return a bunch of cmdlets, that you can go through and understand in-depth. In this section, we will be using some of these cmdlets to query forests, domain, domain controllers, and other details.

Querying forest and domain details

Forests and domains are high-level logical entities in Active Directory. We can get the details of the current domain using the Get-ADDomain cmdlet. Running the following command without any parameters will return the current domain details:

```
Get-ADDomain
```

The previous command will return details such as the DNS name of the domain, the NetBIOS name, default container details of users, computers, deleted objects, child domains, parent domain details, **Group Policy Objects (GPOs)** linked at the domain level, domain mode, and much more. Try this command in your lab setup to check the details that it returns.

Similarly, the Get-ADForest command will return details about the forest from PowerShell to the server or domain controller you are running from. Look at the following output where Get-ADForest retrieved details about current forest details:

```
PS C:\> Get-ADForest
ApplicationPartitions : {DC=DomainDnsZones,DC=techibee,DC=ad,
  DC=ForestDnsZones,DC=techibee,DC=ad}
CrossForestReferences : {}
DomainNamingMaster    : TIBDC2.techibee.ad
Domains               : {sales.techibee.ad, techibee.ad}
ForestMode            : Windows2012Forest
GlobalCatalogs        : {WIN-GU0PBL7NKSG.techibee.ad,
  TIBDC2.techibee.ad}
Name                  : techibee.ad
PartitionsContainer   :
  CN=Partitions,CN=Configuration,DC=techibee,DC=ad
RootDomain            : techibee.ad
SchemaMaster          : TIBDC2.techibee.ad
```

```
Sites                    : {DEFAULT, SNG, INDIA}

SPNSuffixes              : {}

UPNSuffixes              : {}


PS C:\>
```

This will help you to understand current forest configuration details, such as a list of domains and sites in the current forest, forest level operation master roles, and other similar details.

Querying domain controller details

Domain Controllers (DCs) are the actual servers that hold domain information and replicate the data among themselves. DC details can be queried using the `Get-ADDomainController` cmdlet, which can get the details of a Domain Controller when the name or any other identity is provided; it is also capable of getting the DC that matches given criteria.

Now, let's see the details of a domain controller named `TIBDC2` using the following command:

```
Get-ADDomainController -Identity TIBDC2
```

The following screenshot shows the list of details returned by the cmdlet when queried by a DC directly by identity:

```
PS C:\> Get-ADDomainController -Identity TIBDC2

ComputerObjectDN         : CN=TIBDC2,OU=Domain Controllers,DC=techibee,DC=ad
DefaultPartition         : DC=techibee,DC=ad
Domain                   : techibee.ad
Enabled                  : True
Forest                   : techibee.ad
HostName                 : TIBDC2.techibee.ad
InvocationId             : eb8cb916-2b11-4189-81e9-99d30a928333
IPv4Address              : 10.10.101.10
IPv6Address              :
IsGlobalCatalog          : True
IsReadOnly               : False
LdapPort                 : 389
Name                     : TIBDC2
NTDSSettingsObjectDN     : CN=NTDS Settings,CN=TIBDC2,CN=Servers,CN=INDIA,CN=Sites,CN=Configuration,DC=techibee,DC=ad
OperatingSystem          : Windows Server 2012 R2 Standard Evaluation
OperatingSystemHotfix    :
OperatingSystemServicePack :
OperatingSystemVersion   : 6.3 (9600)
OperationMasterRoles     : {SchemaMaster, DomainNamingMaster}
Partitions               : {DC=ForestDnsZones,DC=techibee,DC=ad, DC=DomainDnsZones,DC=techibee,DC=ad,
                           CN=Schema,CN=Configuration,DC=techibee,DC=ad, CN=Configuration,DC=techibee,DC=ad...}
ServerObjectDN           : CN=TIBDC2,CN=Servers,CN=INDIA,CN=Sites,CN=Configuration,DC=techibee,DC=ad
ServerObjectGuid         : ea62a8aa-6e84-4dad-8cdf-f98254563e01
Site                     : INDIA
SslPort                  : 636


PS C:\>
```

You can find all domain controllers in the current domain using the following command:

```
Get-ADDomainController -Filter * | select Hostname
```

All domain controllers in the current forest can be listed using the following piece of code:

```
function Get-DCDetails {
[cmdletbinding()]
$Domains = (Get-ADForest).Domains
foreach($Domain in $Domains) {
    $DCs = Get-ADDomainController -Filter * -Server $Domain
foreach ($DC in $DCs) {
        $OutputObj = New-Object -TypeName PSobject
  $OutputObj | Add-Member -MemberType NoteProperty -Name DCName -
  Value $DC.HostName
  $OutputObj | Add-Member -MemberType NoteProperty -Name SITE -
  Value $DC.SITE
  $OutputObj | Add-Member -MemberType NoteProperty -Name Domain -
  Value $Domain.ToUpper()
  $OutputObj | Add-Member -MemberType NoteProperty -Name IsGC -
  Value $DC.IsGlobalCatalog
  $OutputObj | Add-Member -MemberType NoteProperty -Name IsRODC -
  Value $DC.IsReadOnly
  $OutputObj
    }
}
}
```

This is a simple PowerShell function, that you can copy and paste into PowerShell; you can then call the function by its name.

Running the preceding code will return the name of the Domain Controller, the domain to which it belongs, and the name of the site where the Domain Controller currently resides. This also tells us whether a given DC is a global catalog sever or not and whether it is a **Read-Only Domain Controller (RODC)** or not. This is shown in the following screenshot:

```
PS C:\> Get-DCDetails | ft -AutoSize

DCName                    SITE    Domain          IsGC IsRODC
------                    ----    ------          ---- ------
TIBDC3.sales.techibee.ad  INDIA   SALES.TECHIBEE.AD True False
WIN-GUOPBL7NKSG.techibee.ad DEFAULT TECHIBEE.AD     True False
TIBDC2.techibee.ad        INDIA   TECHIBEE.AD      True False

PS C:\>
```

View the help content of `Get-ADDomainController` to know more use cases. You can get help using the following command:

```
Get-Help Get-ADDomainController -Full
```

This command will display details of each parameter that the cmdlet takes and some of the example codes.

Querying flexible single-master operation role owners

You might have already noticed that `Get-ADDomain` and `Get-ADForest` cmdlet outputs have details about the FSMO role owners. The first one will display domain level roles when the domain name is passed to the `-Server` parameter and, similarly the second one returns forest level roles. So, getting the FSMO role owner details of a given domain is a matter of parsing the output from these two cmdlets for a given domain.

There are several ways to query FSMO roles and the following query is one of them. It is a simple PowerShell function, that you can copy and paste to a PowerShell window; you can then call it by name with the `-DomainName` parameter.

```
Function Get-FSMORoles {
[cmdletbinding()]
param(
    [Parameter(Mandatory=$true)]
    [string]$DomainName
)
try {
    $DomainObj = Get-ADDomain -Server $DomainName -EA Stop
    $ForestObj = Get-ADForest -Server $DomainName -EA Stop
    $OutputObj = New-Object -TypeName PSobject
    $OutputObj | Add-Member -MemberType NoteProperty -Name
    PDCEmulator -Value $DomainObj.PDCEmulator
    $OutputObj | Add-Member -MemberType NoteProperty -Name
    RIDMaster -Value $DomainObj.RIDMaster
    $OutputObj | Add-Member -MemberType NoteProperty -Name
    InfrastructureMaster -Value $DomainObj.InfrastructureMaster
    $OutputObj | Add-Member -MemberType NoteProperty -Name
    SchemaMaster -Value $ForestObj.SchemaMaster
    $OutputObj | Add-Member -MemberType NoteProperty -Name
    DomainNamingMaster -Value $ForestObj.DomainNamingMaster
    $OutputObj
```

```
    } catch {
        Write-Warning "Failed to get Domain details. Verify that it is
        valid domain Name"
    }
}
```

Calling this function is very simple. You can pass the domain name and call it as shown in the following command:

```
PS C:\> Get-FSMORoles -DomainName sales.techibee.ad
PDCEmulator          : TIBDC3.sales.techibee.ad
RIDMaster            : TIBDC3.sales.techibee.ad
InfrastructureMaster : TIBDC3.sales.techibee.ad
SchemaMaster         : TIBDC2.techibee.ad
DomainNamingMaster   : TIBDC2.techibee.ad


PS C:\> Get-FSMORoles -DomainName techibee.ad
PDCEmulator          : WIN-GU0PBL7NKSG.techibee.ad
RIDMaster            : WIN-GU0PBL7NKSG.techibee.ad
InfrastructureMaster : WIN-GU0PBL7NKSG.techibee.ad
SchemaMaster         : TIBDC2.techibee.ad
DomainNamingMaster   : TIBDC2.techibee.ad


PS C:\> Get-FSMORoles -DomainName dummy.techibee.ad
WARNING: Failed to get Domain details. Verify that it is valid domain
    Name
PS C:\>
```

As you will notice in the preceding output, the `Get-FSMORoles` command returned the FMSO roles for domains. This command is also capable of printing a warning message when the given domain name is not found.

Managing Organizational Units

Organizational Units (OUs) are used for grouping various Active Directory objects so that they can be managed easily. In this section, we will look at some of the Active Directory operations related to OUs using PowerShell.

The majority of operations on OUs can be performed using four cmdlets in Active Directory, they are `Get-ADOrganizationalUnit`, `New-ADOrganizationalUnit`, `Set-ADOrganizationalUnit`, and `Remove-ADOrganizationalUnit`. As their names indicate, they are available to perform designated operations. Now, let's look at the usage of these cmdlets by performing some sample operations.

Searching for OUs

In *Chapter 4, Configuring Group Policies,* we used the `Get-ADOrganizationalUnit` cmdlet to get the group policies linked on a given OU. So, from that example, and by looking at the name of the cmdlet, it is clear that this cmdlet can be used to retrieve details of OUs in Active Directory. We can retrieve all kinds of details about an OU using this cmdlet except the objects under the OU.

All OU names in a domain can be queried using the `Get-ADOrganizationalUnit` cmdlet:

```
Get-ADOrganizationalUnit -Filter * | select Name
```

The `-Filter` parameter works in exact way explained in the *Searching and modifying group object information* section of *Chapter 3, Working with Active Directory Groups and Memberships* where we discussed querying AD groups. To query all groups that match a particular string, the `-Filter` parameter can be updated, as shown in the following command:

```
Get-ADOrganizationalUnit -Filter {Name -like "*Servers*" }
```

This command returns all the OUs that have the string servers in their name. Like other AD cmdlets, this one also returns a few properties by default and if you wish see other properties, you can either pass the asterisk (*) symbol to the `-Properties` parameter or the name of the property if you know it in advance, as shown in the following commands:

```
Get-ADOrganizationalUnit -Filter {Name -like "*Servers*" } -
  Properties *
Get-ADOrganizationalUnit -Filter {Name -like "*Servers*" } -
  Properties Name, CreateTimeStamp, ModifyTimeStamp
```

The first command in the preceding example displays all properties of an OU object and the second one displays the name, Creation-Time, and Modification-Time properties of the OU. We can also get the properties of an OU using its **Distinguished Name (DN)** by passing the DN value to the `-Identity` parameter using the following command:

```
Get-ADOrganizationalUnit -Identity "OU=LAB,DC=techibee,DC=ad"
```

The previous result can be achieved by a native method, mentioned in the first chapter. This native method uses **Active Directory Service Interface (ADSI)** adapter to query the Active Directory. ADSI is the accelerator of the `System.DirectoryServices.DirectoryEntry` .Net class as shown in the following command:

```
[ADSI] "LDAP://OU=LAB,DC=techibee,DC=ad" | fl *
```

Running the preceding command returns all the properties of LAB OU. You can see this in the following screenshot:

```
PS C:\> [ADSI]"LDAP://OU=LAB,DC=techibee,DC=ad" | fl *

objectClass                : {top, organizationalUnit}
ou                         : {LAB}
distinguishedName          : {OU=LAB,DC=techibee,DC=ad}
instanceType               : {4}
whenCreated                : {19/6/2014 6:50:38 AM}
whenChanged                : {16/10/2014 6:56:51 PM}
uSNCreated                 : {System.__ComObject}
uSNChanged                 : {System.__ComObject}
name                       : {LAB}
objectGUID                 : {243 183 57 220 97 250 11 64 170 72 49 139 92 169 89 202}
objectCategory             : {CN=Organizational-Unit,CN=Schema,CN=Configuration,DC=techibee,DC=ad}
gPLink                     : {[LDAP://cn={DB5F0BD6-B114-4850-AEB0-88F10D3158DE},cn=policies,cn=system,DC=techibee,DC=a
dSCorePropagationData      : {6/9/2014 11:26:13 AM, 19/6/2014 6:50:39 AM, 19/6/2014 6:50:39 AM, 1/1/1601 12:00:00 AM}
nTSecurityDescriptor       : {System.__ComObject}
AuthenticationType         : Secure
Children                   : {abc, admin1, DaveW, Labuser1...}
Guid                       : f3b739dc61fa0b40aa48318b5ca959ca
ObjectSecurity             : System.DirectoryServices.ActiveDirectorySecurity
NativeGuid                 : f3b739dc61fa0b40aa48318b5ca959ca
NativeObject               : System.__ComObject
Parent                     : LDAP://DC=techibee,DC=ad
Password                   :
Path                       : LDAP://OU=LAB,DC=techibee,DC=ad
Properties                 : {objectClass, ou, distinguishedName, instanceType...}
SchemaClassName            : organizationalUnit
SchemaEntry                : System.DirectoryServices.DirectoryEntry
UsePropertyCache           : True
Username                   :
Options                    : {}
Site                       :
Container                  :

PS C:\>
```

You might see some changes in property names returned by Get-ADOrganizationalUnit and the [ADSI] accelerator. This is because the cmdlet returns the property names in a format that is more user understandable, whereas the [ADSI] accelerator returns the actual attribute names that you see in the adsiedit. msc GUI tool. Look at the following screenshot taken from ADSI editor for LAB OU:

[ADSI] accelerator is useful when you know the exact DN of the OU that you want to query. Otherwise, use the `Get-ADOrganizationalUnit` cmdlet, which is capable of querying the Active Directory by searching for a given OU name. It is also capable of querying OU details by taking a DN as input.

This cmdlet can be used to find child OUs of a given OU. For example, **techibee.ad** lab has an OU called **Prod**, that has three OUs, as shown in the following screenshot:

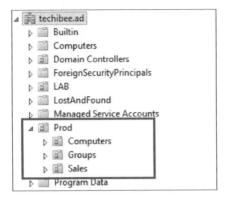

The child OUs of Prod OU can be queried using the following command:

```
Get-ADOrganizationalUnit -Filter * -SearchBase
"OU=Prod,DC=techibee,DC=ad" -SearchScope 1 | select Name ,
DistinguishedName
```

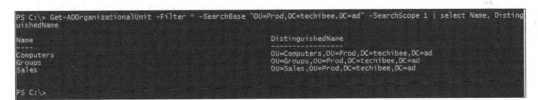

As you can see in the previous screenshot, the command returned the same OUs that you saw in the GUI. In this case, we passed LAB OU `DistinguishedName` as the search base and restricted the search to one level by passing `1` to the `SearchScope` parameter. If you want to query all nested OUs inside the LAB OU, you can do this by changing the `SearchScope` to 2 or by completely removing the `SearchScope` parameter.

Creating OUs

OUs can be created using the `New-ADOrganizationalUnit` cmdlet. The name of the OU is a mandatory parameter for this cmdlet. When this cmdlet is used with just the `-Name` parameter, it creates the OU at the root of the domain. The following example creates a new OU called `Australia Users` inside the LAB OU with the `City` property set to `Sydney`; and the specified description will be added as well, as shown in the following command:

```
New-ADOrganizationalUnit -Name "Australia Users" -Path
    "OU=LAB,DC=techibee,DC=ad" -City Sydney -Description "All user
    accounts of Australia are inside this OU" -
    ProtectedFromAccidentalDeletion $false -PassThru
```

The output in the following screenshot shows that the values we passed to the `New-ADOrganizationalUnit` are reflected in the OU entry that is created:

```
PS C:\> New-ADOrganizationalUnit -Name "Australia Users" -Path "OU=LAB,DC=techibee,DC=ad" -City Sydney -Description "All
user accounts of Australia are inside this OU" -ProtectedFromAccidentalDeletion $false -PassThru

City                    : Sydney
Country                 :
DistinguishedName       : OU=Australia Users,OU=LAB,DC=techibee,DC=ad
LinkedGroupPolicyObjects : {}
ManagedBy               :
Name                    : Australia Users
ObjectClass             : organizationalUnit
ObjectGUID              : 8f23f3fb-53b0-4f0a-b550-5fa560861737
PostalCode              :
State                   :
StreetAddress           :
```

One thing you might notice is the `ProtectedFromAccidentalDeletion` parameter that is set to `$false`. The value of this parameter controls whether protection should be enabled on the newly created OU or not. Starting from Active Directory 2008 R2, a new feature was introduced to prevent accidental deletion or movement of Active Directory Organization Units. This feature is enabled by default on every new OU that you create using Active Directory 2008. So, this is intentionally set to `$false` so that it gets highlighted and you know that it exists.

You can enable or disable this protection feature by accessing the properties of an OU object with **Active Directory Users and Computers (ADUC)** using **Microsoft Management Console (MMC)**. The following screenshot shows the status of protection on the new OU that we just created:

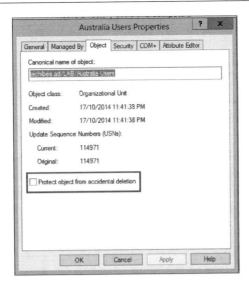

This protection can be enabled or disabled by PowerShell as well; however, we will focus on this when we discuss modifying OUs.

Modifying OUs

The possible changes that we can make to an OU that include changing its name, city, country, description, managed by, and other properties that you can see in the **General** tab of OU properties in ADUC using MMC. The **General** tab of **Australia Users** that we just created is shown in the following screenshot:

Now, let's start working on updating these properties using the Set-ADOrganizationalUnit cmdlet. Before we start modifying the properties of this OU, let's query this object from Active Directory and store it in a variable. Further modifications to this object are made using the following command:

```
$AusOU = Get-ADOrganizationalUnit -Filter "Name -eq 'Australia
    Users'"
```

You have already learned in the previous section about the Get-ADOrganizationalUnit cmdlet, so you know what it does. The $AusOU property will contain the reference to the **Australia Users** OU that we want to modify using the following command:

```
Set-ADOrganizationalUnit -Identity $AusOU -Description "New
    Description added by Set-ADOrganizationalUnit"
```

The preceding command modifies the description of the OU. As you can see, the OU object variable is passed to the -Identity parameter of the Set-ADOrganizationalUnit cmdlet. Similarly, the following command updates the City property to Melbourne from Sydney:

```
Set-ADOrganizationalUnit -Identity $AusOU -City "Melbourne"
```

Country can be updated to Australia in a similar way but the catch here is that it accepts only the two-character country or region code that you want to set. Refer to ISO 3166 (http://www.iso.org/iso/country_codes.htm) for the list of country codes. As per the aforementioned, the country code for Australia is AU as shown in the following command:

```
Set-ADOrganizationalUnit -Identity $AusOU -Country AU
```

The postal code number also can be added in a similar way using the following command

```
Set-ADOrganizationalUnit -Identity $AusOU -PostalCode 3004
```

After making all the previous changes, let's see how the properties of the **Australia Users** OU look. The following screenshot clearly shows that all the changes we made via PowerShell are now visible from ADUC:

The protection feature we talked about earlier can also be turned ON or OFF in a similar way:

```
Set-ADOrganizationalUnit -Identity $AusOU -
  ProtectedFromAccidentalDeletion $true
```

The previous command enables protection on the OU. To disable it, just change the value of the `ProtectedFromAccidentalDeletion` parameter to `$false` from `$true`.

Renaming, moving, and deleting OUs

So far, we have seen how to update the properties of the OU object. Now, let's see how to rename an OU object using PowerShell. We can use the `Rename-ADObject` cmdlet for this purpose, as follows:

```
Rename-ADObject -Identity $AusOU -NewName AustraliaUsers-New
```

The previous command renames the `AustraliaUsers` OU to `AustraliaUsers-New`.

Active Directory OU can be moved from one place to another in the AD logical structure using the Move-ADObject cmdlet. Before you attempt this, be sure to get the object of OU that you want to move. Here, we are not using the same $ausOU variable because we just renamed it. So, we should obtain a fresh reference from AD. To do this, run the same command again but with the new OU name, as shown:

```
$AusOU = Get-ADOrganizationalUnit -Filter "Name -eq
  'AustraliaUsersnew'"
```

After this is done, use the Move-ADObject command to move it to a new location:

```
Move-ADObject -Identity $AusOU -TargetPath
  "OU=PROD,dc=techibee,dc=ad"
```

 You might get an Access Denied message while moving or deleting an Organizational Unit though you are a domain administrator. This is because of the protection feature that is explained earlier. So, be sure to disable this feature before attempting to move or delete.

OUs can be deleted using the Remove-ADOrganizationalUnit cmdlet. Since deletion of an OU is a sensitive operation, this cmdlet prompts for confirmation before deletion. It can be suppressed by setting the -Confirm parameter to $false:

```
Remove-ADOrganizationalUnit -Identity $AusOU -Confirm:$false
```

With this, we have completed management of Organizational Units using PowerShell.

Managing sites and subnets

Sites and subnets play a critical role in controlling authentication traffic and replication traffic in the Active Directory environment. In the same way we managed several logical components of Active Directory, these physical components also can be managed. However, there are no cmdlets available directly in Active Directory module to create and modify sites and subnets such as New-ADSite, Set-ADSite, and so on. We need to write a piece of code to query these objects using the Get-ADObject cmdlet and modify using the Set-ADObject cmdlet.

Querying sites and subnets

Sites and subnets are part of **Configuration Naming Context (CNC)** in Active Directory. By default, the Active Directory cmdlets query the domain naming context where the data of users, computers, groups, and OUs is stored. So, we need to tell the cmdlets to look at CNC to query sites and subnets.

First, we need to get the DN of the CNC partition, so that we can make use of it further in our code, as follows:

```
$ConfigNC=(Get-ADRootDSE).ConFigurationNamingContext
```

As shown in the following screenshot, the $ConfigNC cmdlet will now contain the DN of CNC:

```
Administrator: Windows PowerShell

PS C:\> $ConfigNC = (Get-ADRootDSE).ConFigurationNamingContext
PS C:\> $ConfigNC
CN=Configuration,DC=techibee,DC=ad
PS C:\>
```

Now, we can query for site objects using the Get-ADObject cmdlet by passing the DN of Configuration Naming context to SearchBase:

```
Get-ADObject -Filter {ObjectClass -eq "Site" } -SearchBase $ConfigNC
```

This displays the name of the site, the DN, object class and **Globally Unique Identifier (GUID)** of the sites, as shown in the following screenshot:

```
PS C:\> Get-ADObject -Filter {ObjectClass -eq "Site" } -SearchBase $ConfigNC

DistinguishedName           Name                    ObjectClass        ObjectGUID
-----------------           ----                    -----------        ----------
CN=Default-First-Site-Name... Default-First-Site-Name   site           cebdd031-f67d-43a9-8ea6-b9...
CN=SNG,CN=Sites,CN=Configu... SNG                       site           27991f3f-d41c-41cb-9d61-ba...
CN=INDIA,CN=Sites,CN=Confi... INDIA                     site           fa4c28a7-8c08-4fbc-a4a9-f9...

PS C:\>
```

The -Filter parameter of Get-ADObject can be tuned to search for a particular site, as shown in the following command:

```
Get-ADObject -Filter {ObjectClass -eq "Site" -and Name -eq "INDIA"} -
    SearchBase $ConfigNC
```

This command will return only that site object that has the name INDIA.

Now, if, for example, you are interested in querying all domain controllers in the given site, we can get the site object using the previous command and further use it to get the domain controllers list:

```
$ConfigNC=  (Get-ADRootDSE).ConFigurationNamingContext
```

```
$SiteObj = Get-ADObject -Filter {ObjectClass -eq "Site" -and Name -eq
    "INDIA"} -SearchBase $ConfigNC
```

```
Get-ADObject -Filter {ObjectClass -eq "Server" } -SearchBase
    $SiteObj.DistinguishedName
```

This returns the list of domain controllers in the `INDIA` site. The output includes names of the DC, DN, and the GUID, as we can see in the following screenshot:

There is a script available in *Chapter 9, Miscellaneous Scripts and Resources for Further Learning*, that helps you to list all domain controllers and their site details in one go.

Just as we queried sites, subnets also can be queried using the `Get-ADObject` cmdlet:

```
$ConfigNC=  (Get-ADRootDSE).ConFigurationNamingContext
$SiteObj = Get-ADObject -Filter {ObjectClass -eq "Site" -and Name -eq
  "INDIA"} -SearchBase $ConfigNC -Properties *
$SiteObj.siteObjectBL
```

As you can see in the preceding code, while querying for the site name that matches the string `INDIA`, the `Get-ADObject` cmdlet is requested to return all properties of the found objects. One of the properties of the returned site objects is `siteObjectBL`, which is a backlink object that stores the DN of subnets that are currently mapped to the site.

If you want to see the properties of any of these returned subnets, you can use `Get-ADObject`, as shown in the following command:

```
Get-ADObject -Identity "CN=192.168.0.0/24,CN=Subnets,CN=Sites,
  CN=Configuration,DC=techibee,DC=ad" -Properties *
```

Active Directory module has a cmdlet, `Get-ADReplicationSite`, that can help in querying the site details without much hassle. However, we have used `Get-ADObject` extensively in this section to query sites, so that you can understand how to query any type of object when there are no direct cmdlets available. Similarly, subnet details can be queried using the `Get-ADReplicationSubnet` cmdlet.

Creating and modifying sites

In the previous section, we have seen how to query existing sites and their details. This section talks about creating new sites and modifying their properties. New sites in Active Directory can be created easily using the `New-ADReplicationSite` cmdlet and modifications can be done using `Set-ADReplicationSite`.

Note: These cmdlets are available only in windows 2012 R2 and Windows 8.1

A new site in the existing environment can be easily created using the New-ADReplicationSite cmdlet. Name is a mandatory parameter for this cmdlet and there are a good number of optional parameters that help in setting different configuration parameters of the site, as shown in the following command:

```
New-ADReplicationSite -Name US01
```

You can enable protection, set **Inter-Site Topology Generator (ISTG)**, enable universal group membership caching, and many other options at the time of creation. The following command enables protection and universal group membership caching on the site while creating it:

```
New-ADReplicationSite -Name US01 -ProtectedFromAccidentalDeletion $true
-UniversalGroupCachingEnabled $true
```

 You can refer to the TechNet page at http://technet. microsoft.com/en-us/library/hh852286.aspx to read more about the available options.

To modify the configuration of an already existing site, the Set-ADReplicationSite cmdlet can be used. Several configuration parameters of the site object (and NTDS settings) can be modified using the following cmdlet:

```
Set-ADReplicationSite -Identity US01 -Description "Site created for
United States" -UniversalGroupCachingEnabled $false -PassThru
```

This command adds a description to the site object and disables universal group caching for this site, as shown in the following screenshot:

```
PS C:\> Set-ADReplicationSite -Identity US01 -Description "Site created for United States" -UniversalGroupCachingEnabled
$false -PassThru

Description                        : Site created for United States
DistinguishedName                 : CN=US01,CN=Sites,CN=Configuration,DC=techibee,DC=ad
InterSiteTopologyGenerator        :
ManagedBy                         :
Name                              : US01
ObjectClass                       : site
ObjectGUID                        : dd0b3e30-26c3-4102-81dd-5d8d5b238831
ReplicationSchedule               :
UniversalGroupCachingRefreshSite  :

PS C:\>
```

Creating and modifying subnets

Subnets in Active Directory can be created using the `New-ADReplicationSubnet` cmdlet, much as we created the site. The `-Name` parameter to subnet should be in the network/bits masked format. For example, 172.16.10.0/24. The other optional parameters that can be provided to this cmdlet are site and description. The site is the name of the Active Directory site to which this subnet should be mapped by using the following command:

```
New-ADReplicationSubnet -Name "172.16.10.0/24" -Site US01 -Description
"New IP range in NewYark" -PassThru
```

The `-PassThru` parameter helps in viewing the new object that is created after executing the command, as shown in the following screenshot:

```
PS C:\> New-ADReplicationSubnet -Name "172.16.10.0/24" -Site US01 -Description "New IP range in NewYark" -PassThru

DistinguishedName : CN=172.16.10.0/24,CN=Subnets,CN=Sites,CN=Configuration,DC=techibee,DC=ad
Location          :
Name              : 172.16.10.0/24
ObjectClass       : subnet
ObjectGUID        : 2eb349d3-aed9-47f1-837b-f42e917947cf
Site              : CN=US01,CN=Sites,CN=Configuration,DC=techibee,DC=ad

PS C:\>
```

From the Active Directory sites and services UI, you can see that a new site **US01** is created and the new subnet is mapped to it.

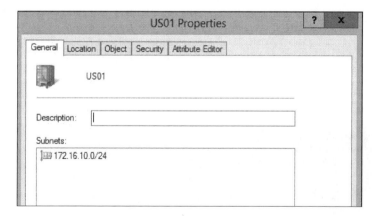

After creating the subnet, we can update its description or it can be remapped to other sites using the `Set-ADReplicationSubnet` cmdlet:

```
Set-ADReplicationSubnet -Identity "172.16.10.0/24" -Description "Subnet
for new building" -Site INDIA
```

The preceding command adds a new description to the subnet object and changes the mapping to the **INDIA** site.

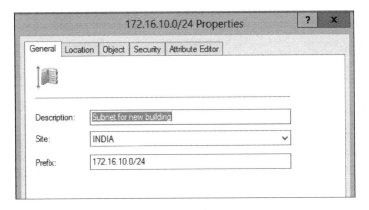

This screenshot shows the status of the subnet object after modifications.

Removing sites and subnets

Removing sites and subnets is very straightforward. `Remove-ADReplicationSite` and `Remove-ADReplicationSubnet` can be used for this purpose:

```
Remove-ADReplicationSite -Identity US01
```

You will receive a warning message similar to the one shown in the following screenshot while attempting to delete a site. It is important to pay attention to such messages and understand the impact before proceeding with the change. In this case, also deleting the Active Directory site can cause problems for domain controllers because the NTDS objects of the domain controllers are children of the site object. It is recommended to delete a site only when it is empty and doesn't have any domain controllers inside it.

```
PS C:\> Remove-ADReplicationSite -Identity US01

Are you sure you want to remove the item and all its children?
Performing recursive remove on Target: 'CN=US01,CN=Sites,CN=Configuration,DC=techibee,DC=ad'.
[Y] Yes  [A] Yes to All  [N] No  [L] No to All  [S] Suspend  [?] Help (default is "Y"):
```

Similarly, AD subnet objects can also be deleted using the following command:

```
Remove-ADReplicationSite -Identity US01
```

Like site deletion, the subnet deletion also prompts for confirmation. Choose the option **YES** after reading through the message. This confirmation message can be skipped by adding `-Confirm:$false` to the previous command.

Summary

In this chapter, we explored various operational exercises related to Active Directory domains, OUs, and sites using PowerShell. These are the stepping stones for further learning. You can explore each cmdlet by querying its help content. This is the best way to improve your knowledge of these cmdlets.

The next chapter covers performing some advanced operations in Active Directory such as installing of new domains and domain controllers, replication management, the transfer of FSMO roles, and so on using PowerShell. Performing these operations helps automate complex tasks.

6

Advanced AD Operations Using PowerShell

As the title suggests, you will learn about performing some of the advanced Active Directory operations using PowerShell in this chapter. Windows administrators who manage Active Directory environments can leverage the contents of this chapter to automate some of these advanced operations and perform troubleshooting. In large complex environments, these operations are pretty frequent and common, which calls for automation to save everyone's time.

While PowerShell can be used for performing many high-level operations in Active Directory, this chapter will focus on the following common and frequently used topics that are helpful to most administrators:

- Installing a new domain
- Adding additional domain controllers
- Obtaining replication status of Active Directory
- Managing fine-grained password policies
- Transferring FSMO roles
- Restoring deleted objects
- Demoting domain controllers and removing domains

Let's see how we can achieve these tasks using PowerShell in the Windows Server 2012 R2 environment. Also, the modules and cmdlets used in this chapter are available on Windows Server 2012 but the demonstration is completely based on its R2 version.

Installing a new domain

Starting from Windows Sever 2012, Microsoft has changed the way Active Directory installations work. It stopped supporting `dcpromo` and now the installation of Active Directory domain or domain controllers is completely through roles in Server Manager. If you run the `dcpromo.exe` command on Windows Server 2012 or later, the following message will appear:

As you can read from the preceding screenshot, the **Active Directory Domain Services installation** has been moved to the **Server Manager** snap-in. It can be installed and configured like any role installation that you do from Server Manager. In this section, we will leverage PowerShell and learn the procedure to perform installation and configuration of the AD DS role. Configuration is nothing but a setting whether you want to create a new domain (or forest) or you want to make the server as domain controller for an existing domain. Configuration also includes topics such as where you want to place the DIT file, logs, SYSVOL, whether it is a **Read Only Domain Controller (RODC)**, details of the server from where you want to perform the initial replication, and so on.

Installation of the AD DS role is very simple and straightforward. The `Install-WindowsFeature` cmdlet in the `ServerManager` PowerShell module helps with installation. Let's first find the status of the role on the server on which we want to perform the installation. In this demonstration, we are going to install a new domain called `techibee.local` on `TIBDC4`. It is the first domain controller in the domain.

First, import the `ServerManager` module using the following cmdlet into the current PowerShell session:

```
Import-Module ServerManager
```

Once imported, we can start the installation of AD DS Role using the `Install-WindowsFeature` cmdlet in the `ServerManager` module, as shown in the following command:

```
PS C:\>Install-WindowsFeature -Name AD-Domain-Services
-IncludeManagementTools| fl
```

```
Success        : True

RestartNeeded : No

FeatureResult : {Active Directory Domain Services, Remote Server
   Administration Tools, Active Directory module forWindows
   PowerShell, AD DS and AD LDS Tools...}

ExitCode       : Success

PS C:\>
```

When the preceding command is executed, you will see the PowerShell progress bar at the top of the PowerShell window. As you can see in the output, the command installed a few additional features along with the AD DS Role. These are the essential components for configuring AD DS from PowerShell and are also required for configuring AD DS using UI components.

The preceding installation provides a new Active Directory module called ADDSDeployment, that contains cmdlets for performing several deployment tasks related to Active Directory.

The following command shows the available commands in the ADDSDeployment module:

```
Get-Command -Module ADDSDeployment
```

The following screenshot shows output of the preceding command:

```
PS C:\> Get-Command -Module ADDSDeployment

CommandType     Name                                               ModuleName
-----------     ----                                               ----------
Cmdlet          Add-ADDSReadOnlyDomainControllerAccount            ADDSDeployment
Cmdlet          Install-ADDSDomain                                 ADDSDeployment
Cmdlet          Install-ADDSDomainController                       ADDSDeployment
Cmdlet          Install-ADDSForest                                 ADDSDeployment
Cmdlet          Test-ADDSDomainControllerInstallation              ADDSDeployment
Cmdlet          Test-ADDSDomainControllerUninstallation            ADDSDeployment
Cmdlet          Test-ADDSDomainInstallation                        ADDSDeployment
Cmdlet          Test-ADDSForestInstallation                        ADDSDeployment
Cmdlet          Test-ADDSReadOnlyDomainControllerAccountCreation   ADDSDeployment
Cmdlet          Uninstall-ADDSDomainController                     ADDSDeployment

PS C:\> _
```

This section completely relies on the preceding cmdlets to configure Active Directory environment.

As we want to install a new forest (`techibee.local`), we need to choose `Install-ADForest` from the preceding list of cmdlets. Before we proceed with the installation, we need to identify a few details that are essential for new domain installation. One has to do this irrespective of whether PowerShell or GUI is used for installation. The details of the new domain installation are as follows:

- **Domain FQDN and NetBIOS name**: Decide the FQDN, which is short for Fully Qualified Domain Name (For example, techibee.local), you want to keep for the domain and the NetBIOS name. The domain name is mandatory and the NetBIOS name is optional. When a NetBIOS name is not specified, it is computed from the domain name. In this demonstration, we are setting the domain name to techibee.local and NetBIOS name to TIBROOT.

- **Domain mode and forest mode**: Decide on the domain mode and forest mode that you want to set for the new domain. Available domain and forest modes are Win2003, Win2008, Win2008R2, Win2012, and Win2012R2. If you don't specify a mode, it is computed and configured automatically. In this demonstration, we are setting the domain and forest levels to the highest (Win2012R2).

- **Database path, Logs path, and SYSVOL path**: By default, these logs are placed in the system root folder (for example, `C:\Windows`). However, some organizations prefer to have them in different locations than the default. In such cases, create the folders well in advance before you pass them to the cmdlet. Executing the command will not create the folders. In this demonstration, we will keep them in a folder called `C:\ADDS`.

- **Safe mode Admin Password**: This is also called as **Directory Service Recovery Mode (DSRM)** password. This is the password that you need to enter when you boot your domain controller in AD DS Recovery mode. Decide on a password and it should be passed as a secure string to the `Install-ADForest` cmdlet.

Once you have these details ready, you can proceed with installing a new domain in the forest using the `Install-ADForest` cmdlet.

There are two commands that install the new domain:

- The following command prompts for the DSRM password. Enter the password that you have chosen:

```
$dsrmpwd = Read-Host "Enter DSRM Password" -AsSecureString
```

- The following command installs the Active Directory domain called `techibee.local`:

```
Install-ADDSForest -DomainNametechibee.local -
  DomainNetbiosName TIBROOT -DomainMode Win2012R2 -ForestMode
  Win2012R2 -SafeModeAdministratorPassword $dsrmpwd -
  InstallDns -DatabasePath C:\ADDS\DS_DB_Logs -LogPath
  C:\ADDS\DS_DB_Logs -SysvolPath C:\ADDS\SYSVOL -
  NoRebootOnCompletion
```

Here is the output, showing a few warning messages; they are mostly related to the domain and forest mode that was chosen, and about creation of DNS delegation, as shown in the following screenshot:

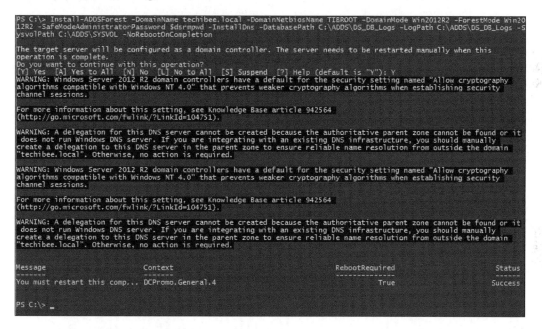

You should carefully read these warnings and understand if any action is required or if they affect you in anyway.

The **Status** column in the end result shows the installation status. A `Success` value indicates that the first domain in the new forest is successfully deployed. The **Message** column shows that the server should be rebooted to make the changes come into effect.

After the reboot, you can get details of forest and domain using the commands you learned in *Chapter 5, Managing Domains, OrganizationalUnits, Sites and Subnets*, which are as follows:

`Get-ADForest`

`Get-ADDomain`

After the completion of these commands, review any warning or error messages for necessary actions. The **Status** column in the output indicates the installation status. If everything looks good, then proceed with installation of the server so that the configuration can come into effect. Reboot can be automated by omitting the `-NoRebootOnCompletion` parameter but this will not give us a chance to review the output of the command.

This completes installation of the first domain in the forest. If you would like to add additional domain controllers to this domain, you can do so using the `Install-ADDSDomainController` cmdlet. The next section in this chapter helps with the required procedure for adding additional domain controllers to a domain using PowerShell.

If you want to install a new domain in an existing forest, then you can make use of the `Install-ADDSDomain` cmdlet. The parameters for this cmdlet are pretty much common when compared to the `Install-ADDSForest` cmdlet with slight changes. At the time of installation, you need to specify the parent domain name using the `-ParentDomainName` parameter and a few parameters related to DNS delegation.

 You can get complete details about this cmdlet from `http://technet.microsoft.com/en-us/library/hh974722.aspx`.

Adding additional domain controllers

In the previous section, we have seen how to deploy a new domain. Active Directory domains without any redundancy are prone to lots of problems in the environment. So, Windows administrators design their Active Directory environment to be redundant by deploying multiple domain controllers. The necessity to add multiple domain controllers increases on a frequent basis when the load increases or a new office is opened. This section helps you to understand what is required to add additional domain controllers to existing Active Directory environment using PowerShell.

As we have seen earlier, the `Install-ADDSDomainController` cmdlet is available in the `ADDSDeployment` PowerShell module and we can leverage it to build additional DCs. The prerequisite for installing a new DC is installing an AD DS role. You can follow the installation of AD DS roles, which we covered in the previous section. Once you have the AD DS components installed, we can promote it as DC in an existing domain using the `Install-ADDSDomainController` cmdlet, as shown in the following command:

```
PS C:\> Install-ADDSDomainController -DomainName techibee.local -
    SiteName SITE-A -SafeModeAdministratorPassword $DSRMPwd-
    DatabasePath C:\ADDS\DS_DB_Logs -LogPath C:\ADDS\DS_DB_Logs -
    SysvolPath C:\ADDS\SYSVOL -InstallDns -NoRebootOnCompletion -
    ReplicationSourceDC TIBDC4.techibee.local -Credential (Get-
    Credential)
```

You should carefully review the warning messages or any errors messages that you encounter after executing this command. These messages will have an effect on functions that this domain controller can serve and the output you get after you execute this command is as shown in the following screenshot:

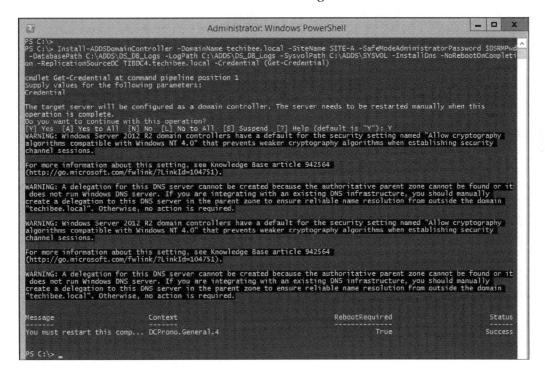

As you might have noticed in the preceding screenshot, the command will add TIBDC5 servers as a DC in an existing domain with database, log files, and SYSVOL folders placed at a custom location. It places this new DC in an Active Directory site, SITE-A, using the `-SiteName` parameter. Also, it installs DNS as part of the DC installation using the `-InstallDNS` parameter. The `-ReplicationSourceDC` parameter tells the new DC where it should replicate the data from. If you are doing a media-based installation in offices where you have poor network connectivity, then you can use the `-InstallationMediaPath` parameter to provide the path of a backup file.

Another thing to note here is the `-Credential` parameter, which is used in the preceding command. Since the DC we are installing is currently in a workgroup, the command needs a credential to connect to existing DCs in the domain to perform a new domain installation. The credentials we provide to the `-Credential` parameter are used for this purpose. The preceding command will prompt you for the credentials and you will need to enter a domain account, that is capable of adding new DCs to an existing domain. You can also store the credentials in a variable and pass it to this parameter. The `Install-ADDSDomainController` cmdlet has several other options that help you in customizing the installations.

> You can get a full list of supported arguments either by looking at the help content of this cmdlet or from `http://technet.microsoft.com/en-us/library/hh974723.aspx`.

There are a few cmdlets in the `ADDSDeployment` module that help you to verify if your environment is ready for installing a new forest, domain, or additional DC by examining the parameters provided to them. The `Install-ADDSForest`, `Install-ADDSDomain`, and `Install-ADDSDomainController` cmdlets are capable of checking for these prerequisites and display an error if any of them are not met. Though their names sound like they can verify the installation status of a new forest, domain, or DC, their purpose is to just verify the prerequisites for installation. Don't get confused here with the names. However, if you want to check these requisites before you start installing the DC, you can use the following command:

```
Get-Command -Module ADDSDeployment -Name Test*
```

The cmdlets in the following screenshot take the same list of arguments as their `Install-*`cmdlet counterparts and verify if all the provided parameters are correct and valid:

```
PS C:\> Get-Command -Module ADDSDeployment -Name Test*

CommandType     Name                                            ModuleName
-----------     ----                                            ----------
Cmdlet          Test-ADDSDomainControllerInstallation           ADDSDeployment
Cmdlet          Test-ADDSDomainControllerUninstallation         ADDSDeployment
Cmdlet          Test-ADDSDomainInstallation                     ADDSDeployment
Cmdlet          Test-ADDSForestInstallation                     ADDSDeployment
Cmdlet          Test-ADDSReadOnlyDomainControllerAccountCreation ADDSDeployment


PS C:\> _
```

For example, the `Test-ADDSDomainControllerInstallation` cmdlet takes the same set of arguments as the `Install-ADDSDomainController` cmdlet and verifies if all the provided parameters are valid. It tests whether the `C:\ADDS\DS_DB_Logs` folder exists and whether the site name you chose exists; it also checks the ability to communicate with DCs in the domain using the credentials you provided and executes various checks. It gives a meaningful error message when any of these checks fails.

> Note: If you have already verified the prerequisites with the `Test-ADDSDomainControllerInstallation` cmdlet and don't want the checks to be run at the time of DC installation, you can skip it by passing the `-SkipPreChecks` parameter with the `Install-ADDSDomainController` cmdlet.

Obtaining an Active Directory replication status

In Active Directory, replication is crucial. Any replication failures can cause inconsistency and might provide different results to different set of users. Because of this reason, organizations have tight controls around monitoring Active Directory replication failures and consistency. Windows administrators rely on the most famous utility, `repadmin.exe`, to query the replication data. It provides very detailed information about the replication status between domain controllers and metadata details of DCs, objects, and so on. However, developing automations around the `repadmin.exe` utility is not so easy because the output is in text format and you need to parse it to get the required portion of data. Given these reasons, Microsoft has introduced a few cmdlets in the Active Directory module starting from Windows Server 2012 to deal with Active Directory replication. This list is not exhaustive enough to perform all sorts of replication activities but serves common needs.

To get all cmdlets that work with replication in Active Directory, you can use the following command:

```
Get-Command -Module ActiveDirectory -Name *repl*
```

As you can see in the following screenshot, there are a few cmdlets that work with Active Directory sites, subnets, and links:

```
PS C:\> Get-Command -Module ActiveDirectory -Name *repl*

CommandType     Name                                                ModuleName
-----------     ----                                                ----------
Cmdlet          Add-ADDomainControllerPasswordReplicationPolicy     ActiveDirectory
Cmdlet          Get-ADAccountResultantPasswordReplicationPolicy     ActiveDirectory
Cmdlet          Get-ADDomainControllerPasswordReplicationPolicy     ActiveDirectory
Cmdlet          Get-ADDomainControllerPasswordReplicationPolicy...  ActiveDirectory
Cmdlet          Get-ADReplicationAttributeMetadata                  ActiveDirectory
Cmdlet          Get-ADReplicationConnection                         ActiveDirectory
Cmdlet          Get-ADReplicationFailure                            ActiveDirectory
Cmdlet          Get-ADReplicationPartnerMetadata                    ActiveDirectory
Cmdlet          Get-ADReplicationQueueOperation                     ActiveDirectory
Cmdlet          Get-ADReplicationSite                               ActiveDirectory
Cmdlet          Get-ADReplicationSiteLink                           ActiveDirectory
Cmdlet          Get-ADReplicationSiteLinkBridge                     ActiveDirectory
Cmdlet          Get-ADReplicationSubnet                             ActiveDirectory
Cmdlet          Get-ADReplicationUpToDatenessVectorTable            ActiveDirectory
Cmdlet          New-ADReplicationSite                               ActiveDirectory
Cmdlet          New-ADReplicationSiteLink                           ActiveDirectory
Cmdlet          New-ADReplicationSiteLinkBridge                     ActiveDirectory
Cmdlet          New-ADReplicationSubnet                             ActiveDirectory
Cmdlet          Remove-ADDomainControllerPasswordReplicationPolicy  ActiveDirectory
Cmdlet          Remove-ADReplicationSite                            ActiveDirectory
Cmdlet          Remove-ADReplicationSiteLink                        ActiveDirectory
Cmdlet          Remove-ADReplicationSiteLinkBridge                  ActiveDirectory
Cmdlet          Remove-ADReplicationSubnet                          ActiveDirectory
Cmdlet          Set-ADReplicationConnection                         ActiveDirectory
Cmdlet          Set-ADReplicationSite                               ActiveDirectory
Cmdlet          Set-ADReplicationSiteLink                           ActiveDirectory
Cmdlet          Set-ADReplicationSiteLinkBridge                     ActiveDirectory
Cmdlet          Set-ADReplicationSubnet                             ActiveDirectory

PS C:\> _
```

We have already discussed the usage of sites and subnet-related cmdlets in *Chapter 5, Managing Domains, Organizational Units, Sites, and Subnets*. So in this section, we will concentrate on cmdlets listed in the following table that are actually related to replication of Active Directory data:

Get-ADReplicationAttributeMetadata	Gets the replication metadata for one or more specified attributes of a given object
Get-ADReplicationFailure	Gets details of data mentioning Active Directory replication failure
Get-ADReplicationPartnerMetadata	Gets the replication metadata details for a set of one or more replication partners specified
Get-ADReplicationQueueOperation	Returns replication queue details for a specified server, that is, the Active Directory domain controller. If the queue is 0 (zero) no output is returned in the console

Let's look at each of these cmdlets and their use cases as shown in the
following command:

`Get-ADReplicationAttributeMetadata`:

This cmdlet is useful in retrieving the replication metadata details of a given object
at attribute level. For demonstration purposes, description of a user account called
DaveW is updated on the `WIN-GU0PBL7NKSG` domain controller. Now, let's see how
the metadata values look for the description attribute change.

When the command queries the metadata information from the `WIN-GU0PBL7NKSG`
domain controller, it appears as shown in the following command:

```
PS C:\>Get-ADReplicationAttributeMetadata -Filter * -Object (Get-
    ADUser -Identity DaveW) -Server localhost | sort
    LastOriginatingChangeTime | select -Last 1
```

```
AttributeName                                       : description
AttributeValue                                      : Finance User
FirstOriginatingCreateTime                          :
IsLinkValue                                         : False
LastOriginatingChangeDirectoryServerIdentity        : CN=NTDS
    Settings,CN=WIN-GU0PBL7NKSG,CN=Servers,CN=DEFAULT,CN=Sites,
    CN=Configuration,DC=techibee,DC=ad
LastOriginatingChangeDirectoryServerInvocationId : 85e00f3b-e233-
    48aa-9c1d-7485a3f014ab
LastOriginatingChangeTime                           : 3/11/2014
    1:47:09 AM
LastOriginatingChangeUsn                            : 157462
LastOriginatingDeleteTime                           :
LocalChangeUsn                                      : 157462
Object                                              :
    CN=DaveW,OU=LAB,DC=techibee,DC=ad
Server                                              : WIN-
    GU0PBL7NKSG.techibee.ad
Version                                             : 3
PS C:\>
```

When queried from the other domain controller, `TIBDC2`, the attribute metadata information appears as shown in the following command:

```
PS C:\>Get-ADReplicationAttributeMetadata -Filter * -Object (Get-
  ADUser -Identity DaveW) -Server TIBDC2 | sort
  LastOriginatingChangeTime | select -Last 1
```

```
AttributeName                                        : description

AttributeValue                                       : Finance User

FirstOriginatingCreateTime                           :

IsLinkValue                                          : False

LastOriginatingChangeDirectoryServerIdentity         : CN=NTDS
  Settings,CN=WIN-GU0PBL7NKSG,CN=Servers,CN=DEFAULT,CN=Sites,
  CN=Configuration,DC=techibee,DC=ad

LastOriginatingChangeDirectoryServerInvocationId : 85e00f3b-e233-
  48aa-9c1d-7485a3f014ab

LastOriginatingChangeTime                            : 3/11/2014
  1:47:09 AM

LastOriginatingChangeUsn                             : 157462

LastOriginatingDeleteTime                            :

LocalChangeUsn                                       : 58159

Object                                               :
  CN=DaveW,OU=LAB,DC=techibee,DC=ad

Server                                               :
  TIBDC2.techibee.ad

Version                                              : 3

PS C:\>
```

As you can see in both cases, we are querying the attribute metadata information of the `DaveW` user account, sorting by the `LastOriginatingChangeTime` value and showing the last result. In both cases, you can see that the description value is set to `Finance User` and the change is originated at `WIN-GU0PBL7NKSG`. The information provided by this cmdlet is useful for troubleshooting or investigating attribute changes of any Active Directory object.

The following cmdlet shows the replication status of one or multiple domain controllers. It also indicates how many times the replication failed and the starting time of the failures:

```
Get-ADReplicationFailure:
```

The following command shows that WIN-GU0PBL7NKSG has replication issues since the last two attempts with its partner TIBDC2:

```
PS C:\>Get-ADReplicationFailure -Target WIN-GU0PBL7NKSG
```

```
FailureCount     : 2

FailureType      : Link

FirstFailureTime : 2/11/2014 5:14:40 PM

LastError        : 1256

Partner          : CN=NTDS Settings,CN=TIBDC2,CN=Servers,
    CN=INDIA,CN=Sites,CN=Configuration,DC=techibee,DC=ad

PartnerGuid      : 9bd89086-4636-4f04-bc20-8728c76a860f

Server           : WIN-GU0PBL7NKSG.techibee.ad

PS C:\>
```

This DC was offline for some time and hence we are seeing these failures. If we make the DC online and force the replication, you should see the FailureCount reverting to 0. The -Target parameter of this cmdlet by default assumes that you provided the name of a domain controller. However, you can provide a site name, domain name, or a forest name to get the replication errors from all domain controllers in that scope. In such cases, you need to specify the -Scope parameter and also specify what kind of object you passed to the -Target parameter (for example, site, domain, and forest).

Following are sample commands, that help in querying the replication failures in site, domain, and forest:

- This command queries all the domain controllers in the techibee.ad forest for replication failures:

  ```
  Get-ADReplicationFailure  -Target techibee.ad -scope Forest
  ```

- This command queries all the domain controllers in the techibee.ad domain for replication failures:

  ```
  Get-ADReplicationFailure  -Target techibee.ad -scope Domain
  ```

- This command queries all the domain controllers in the INDIA site for replication failures:

  ```
  Get-ADReplicationFailure  -Target INDIA -scope Site
  ```

You can have a daily script based on this cmdlet to query replication failures in your Active Directory environment. Having such a check helps in detecting replication problems well before someone reports them.

The following cmdlet returns the metadata information of the replication partner of a given domain controller:

```
Get-ADReplicationPartnerMetadata:
```

The information includes the last replication attempt time, status, partner invocation ID, GUID, details of the partition it is replicating, type transport link (IP/SMTP), compression status of replication, and so on.

The following command will give you the partner's metadata information from all domain controllers in domain:

```
Get-ADReplicationPartnerMetadata -Target *
```

If you are looking for this information from a specific domain controller, then you can specify the name of the DC, as shown in the following command:

```
PS C:\>Get-ADReplicationPartnerMetadata -Target TIBDC2
```

```
CompressChanges                  : True
ConsecutiveReplicationFailures   : 0
DisableScheduledSync             : False
IgnoreChangeNotifications        : False
IntersiteTransport               :
IntersiteTransportGuid           :
IntersiteTransportType           : IP
LastChangeUsn                    : 157462
LastReplicationAttempt           : 3/11/2014 2:01:15 AM
LastReplicationResult            : 0
LastReplicationSuccess           : 3/11/2014 2:01:15 AM
Partition                        : DC=techibee,DC=ad
PartitionGuid                    : 93cecb73-8da2-468e-96bf-
   dfd208e3aa2a
Partner                          : CN=NTDS Settings,CN=WIN-
   GU0PBL7NKSG,CN=Servers,CN=DEFAULT,CN=Sites,CN=Configuration,DC
   =techibee,DC=ad
PartnerAddress                   : 85e00f3b-e233-48aa-9c1d-
   7485a3f014ab._msdcs.techibee.ad
```

```
PartnerGuid                  : 85e00f3b-e233-48aa-9c1d-
   7485a3f014ab

PartnerInvocationId          : 85e00f3b-e233-48aa-9c1d-
   7485a3f014ab

PartnerType                  : Inbound

ScheduledSync                : True

Server                       : TIBDC2.techibee.ad

SyncOnStartup                : True

TwoWaySync                   : False

UsnFilter                    : 157462

Writable                     : True


PS C:\>
```

You can see that this cmdlet returns the details that are mentioned earlier. This information is helpful in troubleshooting replication issues between domain controllers.

The following cmdlet returns the replication tasks that are currently queued on a domain controller:

`Get-ADReplicationQueueOperation:`

For example, if you imitate replication from DC1 to DC2, you can run this cmdlet against DC2 to verify if the replication task is added to the queue or not. The items will be removed from the replication queue of the domain controller once the items processed. One thing to note here is that it doesn't say whether the item in the replication queue completed successfully or failed. It just displays the list of replication tasks pending in a domain controller.

The following command is a sample output from the WIN-GU0PBL7NKSG domain controller, which has replication items from TIBDC2 in the queue:

```
PS C:\>Get-ADReplicationQueueOperation -Server WIN-GU0PBL7NKSG

EnqueueTime    : 5/11/2014 7:55:33 PM

OperationID    : 1050

OperationType  : Sync

Options        : 4099

Partition      : DC=techibee,DC=ad

Partner        : CN=NTDS Settings,CN=TIBDC2,CN=Servers,
   CN=INDIA,CN=Sites,CN=Configuration,DC=techibee,DC=ad

PartnerAddress : 9bd89086-4636-4f04-bc20-
   8728c76a860f._msdcs.techibee.ad
```

```
Priority        : 90
Server          : WIN-GU0PBL7NKSG.techibee.ad
PS C:\>
```

This command can be executed against all domain controllers in the domain to know if there is a large number of items stuck in the queue, causing issues. The output of this cmdlet is the same as what you see when you run the `repadmin` command:

```
Repadmin.exe /queue
```

The preceding command displays the queued replication requests on the domain controller from where you run this. The advantage of the `Get-ADReplicationQueueOperation` cmdlet when compared to the preceding command is that it can run remotely against a domain controller and it can be used to check the queue status easily in the middle of a script.

Managing Fine-Grained Password Policies

Fine-Grained Password Policies (FGPP) was introduced with Windows Server 2008 Active Directory to facilitate multiple password policies in domains. Until this was introduced, whichever password policy was set in the default domain controller was to be applied for all domain user accounts, without any exceptions or customization options. If any category of people in a domain wished to tighten or relax password policies, then they needed to be moved to a separate domain because of the limitation with password policies. The introduction of fine-grained policies helped in such situations. This new feature allows creation of separate password policies for a list of users or groups without moving them to different domain.

 You can read more about fine-grained password policies at http://technet.microsoft.com/en-us/library/ cc770394%28v=ws.10%29.aspx.

In this section, let's find out how to query, create, and modify these FGPP. FGPPs are stored in a system container in the domain structure inside a container called **Policy Settings Container (PSC)**. The PSC contains **Password Settings Objects (PSO),** which are nothing but another type of object in Active Directory, similar to user objects or computer objects. These PSOs will have attributes that indicate various settings for password policies. One of the attribute is PSO link, which is a multivalued attribute that links to user objects or group objects to which the policy will be applied.

FGPPs can be managed in two ways. One way is using the `Get-ADObject` and `Set-ADObject` cmdlets in Active Directory and the second way is using the cmdlets that are explicitly designed to work with FGPPs. In both the cases, we are relying on Active Directory module for management. Let's explore cmdlets that are already available for managing fine-grained policies.

The following command shows the list of cmdlets that help in managing FGPPs:

```
Get-Command -Module ActiveDirectory -Name *FineGrainedPassword*
```

The cmdlet list returned by the preceding command is more than sufficient to perform any kind of operations on FGPPs, as shown in the following screenshot:

```
PS C:\> Get-Command -Module ActiveDirectory -Name *FineGrainedPassword*

CommandType     Name                                          ModuleName
-----------     ----                                          ----------
Cmdlet          Add-ADFineGrainedPasswordPolicySubject        ActiveDirectory
Cmdlet          Get-ADFineGrainedPasswordPolicy               ActiveDirectory
Cmdlet          Get-ADFineGrainedPasswordPolicySubject        ActiveDirectory
Cmdlet          New-ADFineGrainedPasswordPolicy               ActiveDirectory
Cmdlet          Remove-ADFineGrainedPasswordPolicy            ActiveDirectory
Cmdlet          Remove-ADFineGrainedPasswordPolicySubject     ActiveDirectory
Cmdlet          Set-ADFineGrainedPasswordPolicy               ActiveDirectory


PS C:\>
```

First, let's find out what are the available FGPPs are in the current domain using following command:

```
PS C:\>Get-ADFineGrainedPasswordPolicy -Filter *
```

```
AppliesTo                 : {CN=SpecialAccounts,CN=Users,
    DC=techibee,DC=local}

ComplexityEnabled         : True

DistinguishedName         : CN=SpecialAccountsPWDPolicy,
    CN=Password Settings Container,CN=System,DC=techibee,DC=local

LockoutDuration           : 00:30:00

LockoutObservationWindow  : 00:30:00

LockoutThreshold          : 0

MaxPasswordAge            : 00:00:00

MinPasswordAge            : 1.00:00:00

MinPasswordLength         : 5

Name                      : SpecialAccountsPWDPolicy

ObjectClass               : msDS-PasswordSettings
```

```
ObjectGUID                    : 9138f24e-b17f-4d80-bda5-dce449333af1
PasswordHistoryCount          : 5
Precedence                    : 1
ReversibleEncryptionEnabled : False


PS C:\>
```

Using the `Get-ADFineGrainedPasswordPolicy` cmdlet we queried the domain for a list of FGPPs and the output shows that there is one such policy that exists with the name `SpecialAccountsPWDPolicy`. The output also shows details about password settings such as lockout threshold, lockout duration, min and max password age, password history count, and precedence of this policy. The output also shows the list of Active Directory objects to which this policy will be applied. We can find more details about the object to which it applies using its DN, as shown in the following command:

```
PS C:\>Get-ADObject -Identity
  "CN=SpecialAccounts,CN=Users,DC=techibee,DC=local"  | fl


DistinguishedName : CN=SpecialAccounts,CN=Users,
  DC=techibee,DC=local
Name               : SpecialAccounts
ObjectClass        : group
ObjectGUID         : d457ea6f-c06f-4d11-911c-b6116ac3bf7b


PS C:\>
```

Modifications to FGPPs can be done using `Set-ADFineGrainedPasswordPolicy`. It has parameters to set most of the password settings that we have seen while querying for FGPPs. In the following example, we are trying to change the minimum password length requirement from five to ten:

```
PS C:\>Set-ADFineGrainedPasswordPolicy -Identity $pwdpolicy -
  MinPasswordLength 10 -PassThru


AppliesTo                     : {CN=SpecialAccounts,CN=Users,
  DC=techibee,DC=local}
ComplexityEnabled             : True
DistinguishedName             : CN=SpecialAccountsPWDPolicy,
  CN=Password Settings Container,CN=System,DC=techibee,DC=local
LockoutDuration               : 00:30:00
```

```
LockoutObservationWindow   : 00:30:00
LockoutThreshold           : 0
MaxPasswordAge             : 00:00:00
MinPasswordAge             : 1.00:00:00
MinPasswordLength          : 10
Name                       : SpecialAccountsPWDPolicy
ObjectClass                : msDS-PasswordSettings
ObjectGUID                 : 9138f24e-b17f-4d80-bda5-dce449333af1
PasswordHistoryCount       : 5
Precedence                 : 1
ReversibleEncryptionEnabled : False
PS C:\>
```

Transferring FSMO roles

In the previous chapter, we have seen how to query FSMO role owners using PowerShell. Instead of relying on the `onnetdom` command or any other method, we leveraged Active Directory PowerShell module and wrote a small PowerShell function, `Get-FSMORoles`, to get this information. In this section, let's concentrate on how to transfer these FSMO roles across domain controllers.

Moving FSMO roles might not be a frequent operation in smaller organizations. However, if you have multiple domains and forests with a large set of domain controllers, generally you see the need to do it on a frequent basis for various reasons. For example, if you have a site where you have a PDC emulator running and there is a power maintenance issue that demands the shutdown of domain controllers, then it makes sense to move the PDC emulator to another DC in a different site.

Active Directory module has a cmdlet called `Move-ADDirectoryServerOperationM asterRole`, which is used for transferring FSMO roles. We need to pass the name of the FSMO role and the name of the domain controller to which you want to transfer the role.

Here is a simple example that transfers the `RIDMaster` role to `TIBDC2` as shown in the following command:

```
PS C:\>Move-ADDirectoryServerOperationMasterRole -Identity TIBDC2 -
    OperationMasterRoleRIDMaster
Move Operation Master Role
```

```
Do you want to move role 'RIDMaster' to server
  'TIBDC2.techibee.ad' ?

[Y] Yes  [A] Yes to All  [N] No  [L] No to All  [S] Suspend  [?]
  Help (default is "Y"): Y

PS C:\>
```

As you can see in the preceding output, this cmdlet prompts for confirmation before performing the operations. You can suppress it using the `-Confirm` parameter with the move command. This command will not display the status of transfer after completion. It will throw errors if there is some issue with the transfer operation. So, you can view the status of role transfer using the `Get-FSMORoles` function, as shown in the following command:

```
PS C:\>Get-FSMORoles -DomainName techibee.ad


PDCEmulator            : WIN-GU0PBL7NKSG.techibee.ad

RIDMaster              : TIBDC2.techibee.ad

InfrastructureMaster : WIN-GU0PBL7NKSG.techibee.ad

SchemaMaster           : TIBDC2.techibee.ad

DomainNamingMaster     : TIBDC2.techibee.ad

PS C:\>
```

This cmdlet can be used for transferring multiple roles at the same time. For example, if you want to transfer all five roles to `TIBDC2`, you can use following command:

```
Move-ADDirectoryServerOperationMasterRole -Identity TIBDC2 -
  OperationMasterRole RIDMaster,PDCEmulator,
  InfrastructureMaster,SchemaMaster,DomainNamingMaster -
  Confirm:$false
```

The preceding command can be further simplified by replacing the role names with numeric numbers, as shown in the following command:

```
Move-ADDirectoryServerOperationMasterRole -Identity TIBDC2 -
  OperationMasterRole 0,1,2,3,4  -Confirm:$false
```

In the preceding command, the numbers 0 to 4 indicate each FSMO role:

- 0: This is the PDCEmulator
- 1: This is the RIDMaster
- 2: This is the InfrastructureMaster
- 3: This is theSchemaMaster
- 4: This is the DomainNamingMaster

This cmdlet also has a parameter called `-Server` for which you can specify the name of the AD DS instance to connect to from where you want to initiate the transfer operation. You can also provide the name of the domain (for example, `sales.techibee.ad`) if the domain from which you are running is different from where you want to perform the transfer.

Can this cmdlet perform the transfer of roles only? Can't it do seizing of the role? Yes, it can do that as well when the `-Force` switch parameter is used. Being a Windows administrator managing Active Directory environments, you know when to perform the transfer and when to opt for seizing. The seize operation is performed when the domain controller holding the FSMO role is permanently offline or down for a longer period due to a hardware failure or crash. Thus, you have to act to seize the role forcefully to the other domain controller.

The following code will demonstrate the `PDCEmulator` seize operation from the `TIBDC2` to the `WIN-GU0PBL7NKSG` domain controller:

First, let's find out the current placement of FSMO Role owners as shown in the following command:

```
PS C:\>Get-FSMORoles -DomainName techibee.ad


PDCEmulator           : TIBDC2.techibee.ad

RIDMaster             : TIBDC2.techibee.ad

InfrastructureMaster  : TIBDC2.techibee.ad

SchemaMaster          : TIBDC2.techibee.ad

DomainNamingMaster    : TIBDC2.techibee.ad


PS C:\>
```

As you can see from the preceding command, all FSMO roles are currently on `TIBDC2`. Now, let's check if `TIBDC2` is reachable or not using the following command:

```
PS C:\>Test-Connection -ComputerName TIBDC2 -Quiet

False
PS C:\>
```

The `False` value in the output indicates that `TIBDC2` is offline. You can also use ping to examine this, but doing it the PowerShell way helps in incorporating the code into scripts.

Now it's time to attempt the seize operation. The following command transfers the role from the TIBDC2 to the WIN-GU0PBL7NKSG domain controller:

```
Move-ADDirectoryServerOperationMasterRole -Identity WIN-GU0PBL7NKSG -
    OperationMasterRolePDCEmulator -Force -Confirm:$false
```

 Notice the -Force switch that is used in the preceding command.

The usage of the -Force switch first attempts to transfer the role in a graceful manner. If this fails, then it attempts to seize the role. Since TIBDC2 is offline, the preceding command seizes the role and places it on the WIN-GU0PBL7NKSG domain controller.

After successful completion of the preceding command, we can verify the status of the seize operation by running the Get-FSMORoles function again, as shown in the following command:

```
PS C:\>Get-FSMORoles -DomainName techibee.ad
PDCEmulator         : WIN-GU0PBL7NKSG.techibee.ad
RIDMaster           : TIBDC2.techibee.ad
InfrastructureMaster : TIBDC2.techibee.ad
SchemaMaster        : TIBDC2.techibee.ad
DomainNamingMaster  : TIBDC2.techibee.ad
PS C:\>
```

As you can see in the output, PDCEmulator role is now transferred to the WIN-GU0PBL7NKSG domain controller.

You can find full details about the Move-ADDirectoryServerOperationMasterRole cmdlet at http://technet.microsoft.com/en-us/library/ee617229.aspx or by running the following command:

```
Get-Help Move-ADDirectoryServerOperationMasterRole -Full
```

This completes your learning about managing FSMO roles using PowerShell. In the next sections, let's look at how to search and restore deleted objects in Active Directory using PowerShell.

Restoring deleted objects

Recovery is important for any IT Infrastructure. Windows administrators perform deletion of users, groups, and computers to clean up stale objects or as part of a user account deprovision process. However, these operations can sometimes cause accidental deletions of live Active Directory objects and in turn affect the business. Recovery is very important in such cases. The faster you can recover these objects, the less impact it can have on the business.

Deleted object recovery till Windows Server 2008 was not a straightforward process and requires time and effort. It includes booting the Active Directory domain controller into **Directory Services Restore Mode (DSRM)** and performing authoritative or non-authoritative restoration of objects.

This situation improved greatly with the introduction of the Optional Recycle Bin feature in Active Directory with Windows Server 2008 R2. With this feature, the recovery process is easy and less time-consuming. One of the prerequisite to enable this feature in Active Directory is that the forest functional level should be at least Windows Server 2008 R2. You can read more about this feature and other details at `http://technet.microsoft.com/en-us/library/dd379484%28v=ws.10%29.aspx`.

The `Enable-ADOptionalFeature` cmdlet in ActiveDirectory module can be used to enable the Recycle Bin feature in Active Directory. You can follow the instructions at `http://technet.microsoft.com/en-us/library/dd379481%28v=ws.10%29.aspx` to enable this feature.

Once you have enabled the Recycle Bin feature and it is working, you can use PowerShell to search for deleted objects easily and recover them. There are two cmdlets that help in searching and restoring Active Directory objects. They are as follows:

- `Get-ADObject`: This helps in searching Active Directory for any object type. It has a switch parameter called `-IncludeDeletedObjects`, that can be used for displaying deleted objects as well if any found during the search operation. Since deleted objects in Active Directory are stored inside a deleted objects container, we need to set the `SearchBase` parameter to its DN.

- `Restore-ADObject`: This cmdlet is used for restoring any deleted object. It takes deleted objects as inputs and can restore to an old location or a new location.

In this section, we will use these two cmdlets to perform search and restore operations on deleted objects. First, let's look at how to find deleted objects using the following command:

```
Get-ADObject -SearchBase "CN=Deleted Objects,DC=techibee,DC=ad"  -
   Filter * -IncludeDeletedObjects | Group-Object -Property
   ObjectClass
```

This command searches for deleted objects inside the CN=Deleted Objects, DC=techibee, and DC=ad containers and lists the objects grouped by their class name. This is shown in the following screenshot:

```
PS C:\> Get-ADObject -SearchBase "CN=Deleted Objects,DC=techibee,DC=ad"  -Filter * -IncludeDeletedObjects | Group-Object
 -Property ObjectClass

Count Name                          Group
----- ----                          -----
    3 container                     {CN=Deleted Objects,DC=techibee,DC=ad, CN=Machine\0ADEL:2c980919-e4f4-4d36-8735-4b60...
    4 computer                      {CN=abc\0ADEL:b0561a40-cefb-4f71-b146-0f23479c1821,CN=Deleted Objects,DC=techibee,DC...
    3 msDFS-NamespaceAnchor         {CN=Projects\0ADEL:2f103edd-b6a4-49b9-bc46-560d3e18fc98,CN=Deleted Objects,DC=techib...
    3 msDFS-Namespacev2             {CN=Projects\0ADEL:e73f24f4-bb58-4bad-918a-ee3d0b6b3d54,CN=Deleted Objects,DC=techib...
    8 msDFS-Linkv2                  {CN=link-b7933dfc-63ce-4f2b-aeac-6ced576a63d2\0ADEL:1c128c64-6815-4f7e-b60f-81c9b8f4...
   11 user                          {CN=Labuser10\0ADEL:62be989c-6431-48bc-9526-c4a7aec285ad,CN=Deleted Objects,DC=techi...
    5 msDFSR-ReplicationGroup       {CN=Scripts\0ADEL:7c1c83fa-ba7b-4099-8a9e-ed0a428c522e,CN=Deleted Objects,DC=techibe...
    5 msDFSR-Topology               {CN=Topology\0ADEL:863a356e-8ed0-4244-ba38-dec818b44909,CN=Deleted Objects,DC=techib...
    5 msDFSR-Content                {CN=Content\0ADEL:a0896e5c-5e90-4744-a2c8-fd6e55605af1,CN=Deleted Objects,DC=techibe...
    8 msDFSR-Member                 {CN=f0aa232d-a3e5-4e52-91ee-db160ed42612\0ADEL:e02b062a-b14f-4270-874e-8f62574811cb,...
    8 msDFSR-Subscriber             {CN=f0aa232d-a3e5-4e52-91ee-db160ed42612\0ADEL:3eb751e2-8de0-4f3d-b3c4-13af1c1d081e,...
    7 msDFSR-ContentSet             {CN=temp\0ADEL:dd4d3e58-3152-407b-848b-86ee4d6bad48,CN=Deleted Objects,DC=techibee,D...
   12 msDFSR-Subscription           {CN=dd4d3e58-3152-407b-848b-86ee4d6bad48\0ADEL:db7564e5-18aa-48fb-b225-582db9993dbc,...
    8 msDFSR-Connection             {CN=efecacdb-a473-4ae6-899e-f4ca69d26e3f\0ADEL:542ea7c4-7c85-4ef9-be02-ac1a3ead381d,...
    1 trustedDomain                 {CN=sales.techibee.ad\0ADEL:5a1e1cf1-83d1-426f-8318-0f091f6ce84e,CN=Deleted Objects,...
    1 serviceConnectionPoint        {CN=Windows Virtual Machine\0ADEL:cd91cfbf-aedd-4c91-9519-0750bff9aeed,CN=Deleted Ob...
    5 organizationalUnit            {OU=Australia Users\0ADEL:6a963338-a59f-4344-ae61-eaa120553145,CN=Deleted Objects,DC...

PS C:\>
```

As you can see in the preceding output, there are 11 user accounts, two containers, four computers, and five Organizational Units found in deleted objects container. Also there are other objects related to DFS and DFS-R but we will focus on working with users, computes, containers, and OUs.

If you don't want to see all object classes and are just interested in user accounts that are in the Recycle Bin, you can use the following command:

```
Get-ADObject -SearchBase "CN=Deleted Objects,DC=techibee,DC=ad"  -
   Filter { ObjectClass -eq "User" } -IncludeDeletedObjects
```

The filter can be further improved if you want to search for a particular user, for example LabUser100 shown in the following command:

```
PS C:\>Get-ADObject -SearchBase "CN=Deleted
   Objects,DC=techibee,DC=ad"  -Filter { ObjectClass -eq "User" -and
   msDS-LastKnownRDN -eq "Labuser100"} -IncludeDeletedObjects  -
   Properties * | select Name, DistinguishedName, Description,
   Deleted, ObjectClass, LastKnownParent
```

```
Name                 : Labuser100
                       DEL:e57d89bf-f585-4fa3-b845-139b56ebc6ad
DistinguishedName : CN=Labuser100\0ADEL:e57d89bf-f585-4fa3-b845-
   139b56ebc6ad,CN=Deleted Objects,DC=techibee,DC=ad
Description          : Finance User
Deleted              : True
ObjectClass          : user
LastKnownParent      : OU=LAB,DC=techibee,DC=ad
PS C:\>
```

In the preceding command, the filter is updated to search for deleted user objects that have the msDS-LastKnownRDN attribute value set to username. This attribute stores the last known display name of the object. In the preceding output, you can notice the values of other properties such as DN, LastKnownParent, description, and so on. The value of the LastKnownParent attributes indicates the location in Active Directory from where this object is deleted.

Similarly, in this way you can search for deleted computer objects or group objects by adjusting the values of the -Filter parameter. Following are the sample commands that you can use for searching other object types:

- Search for deleted computer objects:

```
Get-ADObject -SearchBase "CN=Deleted
   Objects,DC=techibee,DC=ad"  -Filter { ObjectClass -eq
   "Computer"} -IncludeDeletedObjects
```

- Search for deleted group objects:

```
Get-ADObject -SearchBase "CN=Deleted
   Objects,DC=techibee,DC=ad"  -Filter { ObjectClass -eq
   "Group"} -IncludeDeletedObjects
```

- Search for deleted containers or Organizational Units:

```
Get-ADObject -SearchBase "CN=Deleted
   Objects,DC=techibee,DC=ad"  -Filter { ObjectClass -eq
   "Container" -or ObjectClass -eq "organizationalUnit"} -
IncludeDeletedObjects
```

Once we have the object information of the deleted item, we can proceed with restoration using the Restore-ADObject cmdlet. For demonstration, let's restore the LabUser100 user account using the following command:

```
PS C:\>Get-ADObject -SearchBase "CN=Deleted
   Objects,DC=techibee,DC=ad"  -Filter { ObjectClass -eq "User" -and
   msDS-LastKnownRDN -eq "Labuser100"} -IncludeDeletedObjects |
   Restore-ADObject -PassThru | ft -AutoSize
```

The restoration is very simple as shown in the following screenshot:

```
PS C:\> Get-ADObject -SearchBase "CN=Deleted Objects,DC=techibee,DC=ad"  -Filter { ObjectClass -eq "User" -and msDS-Last
KnownRDN -eq "Labuser100"} -IncludeDeletedObjects | Restore-ADObject -PassThru | ft -AutoSize

DistinguishedName                          Name      ObjectClass ObjectGUID
-----------------                          ----      ----------- ----------
cn=Labuser100,OU=LAB,DC=techibee,DC=ad Labuser100 user        e57d89bf-f585-4fa3-b845-139b56ebc6ad


PS C:\>
```

We just need to pass the object of the deleted account to the `Restore-ADobject` cmdlet. The output shows the DN of the user that indicates the path it restored. As mentioned before, it restores to the path that is stored in the `LastKnownDN` attribute of the deleted object. We can verify the status of restoration by querying for the `LabUser100` account using the `Get-ADUser` cmdlet as shown in the following command:

```
PS C:\>Get-ADUser -Identity LabUser100

DistinguishedName  : CN=Labuser100,OU=LAB,DC=techibee,DC=ad
Enabled            : False
GivenName          :
Name               : Labuser100
ObjectClass        : user
ObjectGUID         : e57d89bf-f585-4fa3-b845-139b56ebc6ad
SamAccountName     : Labuser100
SID                : S-1-5-21-822638036-2026389545-1116158610-1351
Surname            :
UserPrincipalName  :

PS C:\>
```

The `Get-ADUser` cmdlet output shows that the object is restored to LAB OU. One thing to note here is that the status of the object will not change after the restoration, which means that all properties of the object stay intact and the password also remains the same.

Also restoration of a deleted object can be performed to a new path using the `-TargetPath` parameter of the `Restore-ADObject` cmdlet. Let's modify the previous restore operation to restore the user object to an OU called PROD, as shown in the following command:

```
Get-ADObject -SearchBase "CN=Deleted Objects,DC=techibee,DC=ad"  -
  Filter { ObjectClass -eq "User" -and msDS-LastKnownRDN -eq
  "Labuser100"} -IncludeDeletedObjects | Restore-ADObject -TargetPath
  "OU=PROD,DC=techibee,DC=AD"
```

The preceding command restores the `LABUser100` user account to the `OU=PROD,DC=techibee,DC=AD` OU. Note that `LABUser100` is deleted again for demonstration purposes. You cannot actually restore an account multiple times. After the restoration to a different path, verify the status of the object by running `Get-ADUser` cmdlet, as shown in the following command:

```
PS C:\>Get-ADUser -Identity LabUser100
```

```
DistinguishedName : CN=Labuser100,OU=Prod,DC=techibee,DC=ad
Enabled           : True
GivenName         :
Name              : Labuser100
ObjectClass       : user
ObjectGUID        : e57d89bf-f585-4fa3-b845-139b56ebc6ad
SamAccountName    : Labuser100
SID               : S-1-5-21-822638036-2026389545-1116158610-1351
Surname           :
UserPrincipalName :
```

```
PS C:\>
```

Now you can see that the object is restored to PROD OU. Restoration of any other deleted computer, group, container, and OU object can be performed in a similar way using the `Restore-ADObject` cmdlet.

Demoting domain controllers and removing domains

At the beginning of this chapter, you saw how to create a new domain (or forest) using PowerShell and also learned how to add new domain controllers to existing domain. Just as we automated this domain or domain controller provision process with the help of cmdlets in the `ADDSDeploy` PowerShell module, we can perform demotion of domain controllers and domains using the cmdlets available in this module.

The cmdlet used for this purpose is `Uninstall-ADDSDomainController`. Using this, we can demote a domain controller alone or the domain (or forest) itself. There is another cmdlet called `Test-ADDSDomainControllerUninstallation`, that helps in verifying prerequisites for uninstalling a domain controller.

When you demote a Windows Server 2012 domain controller manually, you will be prompted with several options that are essential for demotion functionality and later. Following are some of the important parameters that you should understand and have handy to input at the time of domain controller demotion:

- `LocalAdministratorPassword`: This parameter specifies the password to be set for the local administrator account after the demotion of the domain controller.

- `LastDomainControllerInDomain`: This parameter is used for specifying that the domain controller you are demoting is the last domain controller in the domain. If the domain controller being demoted is the last domain controller in a child domain, then you need to use additional parameters such as `Removednsdelegation`, `Removeapplicationpartitions`, `Ignorelastdnsserverforzone`, and so on.

All these parameters (except `LocalAdministratorPassword`) take `$true` or `$false` as a value. So based on the state of the domain controller you demote, decide on the parameters to be used and pass them to the `Test-ADDSDomainControllerUninstallation` cmdlet to ensure that you meet all prerequisites for demoting the domain controller.

The following section demonstrates how to demote additional domain controllers from a domain and demoting the last domain controller in a domain.

First, let's look at how to demote an additional domain controller from a domain. It assumes that you have other domain controllers in this domain running in a healthy condition and reachable.

Since it is an additional domain controller, using the `LocalAdministratorPassword` parameter should be sufficient.

First, read the password into a variable as a secure string so that we can pass it to the `Test-ADDSDomainControllerUninstallation` cmdlet, as shown in the following command:

```
$localadminpassword= Read-Host "Enter password for local admin" -
    AsSecureString
```

Now, we can test whether the domain controller meets all the prerequisites for demoting. This can be done with the following command:

```
Test-ADDSDomainControllerUninstallation -LocalAdministratorPassword
    $localadminpassword
```

If the output shows success, then you are all set to start the demotion process as shown in the following screenshot:

```
PS C:\> Test-ADDSDomainControllerUninstallation -LocalAdministratorPassword $localadminpassword

Message                          Context                                RebootRequired                    Status
-------                          -------                                --------------                    ------
Operation completed succes...    Test.VerifyDcPromoCore.DCP...                    False                    Success

PS C:\>
```

If the Status shows any error, then review the value of the Message property to understand the reason for failures.

To demote the domain controller, use the following command. As you can see it has the same parameters that we passed to the Test cmdlet. Only -NoRebootOnCompletion is used to capture the output after the demotion process:

```
Uninstall-ADDSDomainController -LocalAdministratorPassword
    $localadminpassword -NoRebootOnCompletion
```

When the preceding command is executed, you will be prompted for confirmation, as shown in the following screenshot:

```
PS C:\> Uninstall-ADDSDomainController -LocalAdministratorPassword $localadminpassword -NoRebootOnCompletion

The server needs to be restarted manually when this operation is complete. The domain will no longer exist after you
uninstall Active Directory Domain Services from the last domain controller in the domain.
Do you want to continue with this operation?
[Y] Yes  [A] Yes to All  [N] No  [L] No to All  [S] Suspend  [?] Help (default is "Y"): Y

Message                          Context                                RebootRequired                    Status
-------                          -------                                --------------                    ------
You must restart this comp...    DCPromo.General.2                                 True                    Success

PS C:\>
```

You can suppress it using the -Confirm parameter if you don't want it to prompt. After saying Yes to the confirmation prompt, the demotion process starts and the status message after the completion indicates the results. A success message indicates that demotion is completed successfully. In case of error, review the value of the Message property to find more details about the reason for failures.

This completes the demotion of an additional domain controller in the domain.

Now, let's look at demoting the last domain controller in the domain.

First, we need to test if we have all the prerequisites ready for removing the last domain controller from the domain. Since this domain is a forest root, specifying the LastDomainControllerInDomain and RemoveApplicationPartitions parameters is sufficient. If this is a child domain, then the DNS delegation references from the parent domain DNS should be removed and you need to use the RemoveDNSDelegation and other parameters based on your domain setup. The following command verifies readiness for demoting the last domain controller from the domain:

```
Test-ADDSDomainControllerUninstallation -LocalAdministratorPassword
    $localadminpassword -LastDomainControllerInDomain -
    RemoveApplicationPartitions
```

The output in the following screenshot indicates the cmdlet executed successfully:

```
PS C:\> Test-ADDSDomainControllerUninstallation -LocalAdministratorPassword $localadminpassword -LastDomainControllerInD
omain -RemoveApplicationPartitions

Message                    Context                      RebootRequired                         Status
-------                    -------                      --------------                         ------
Operation completed succes... Test.VerifyDcPromoCore.DCP...              False                 Success

PS C:\> _
```

Since we are good with prerequisites, let's proceed with the actual process for demoting the domain controller by passing the same arguments to the Uninstall-ADDSDomainController cmdlet. The following command will start the uninstallation process and reboots the server after successful completion:

```
Uninstall-ADDSDomainController -LocalAdministratorPassword
    $localadminpassword -LastDomainControllerInDomain -
    RemoveApplicationPartitions -Confirm:$false
```

After the successful completion of this command, you can remove the AD DS role from the server using the Remove-WindowsFeature cmdlet in the ServerManager PowerShell module.

This completes the demonstration of demoting domain controllers and domains using PowerShell in Windows Server 2012 environment. You can find details about manual demotion process of a domain controller at http://technet.microsoft.com/en-us/library/jj574104.aspx.

Summary

In this chapter, we have seen some of the advanced operations in Active Directory and how to perform them using Active Directory and the AD DS Deployment PowerShell modules. The code samples provided in this section help you in kick starting your learning process and improving your skills further. Since these are advanced operations, it is recommended that you understand each parameter that is being used thoroughly and test them in a lab setup before attempting in a production environment.

In the next chapter, we will see how to manage DFS-N (Distributed File System Namespace) and DFS-R (Distributed File System Replication) using PowerShell. To manage these components we need to rely on other modules such as DFS-N and DFS-R in addition to the Active Directory module.

Managing DFS-N and DFS-R Using PowerShell

DFS-N stands for **Distributed File System Namespace** and **DFS-R** stands for **Distributed File System Replication**. These are two familiar technologies for any Windows administrator. DFS-N provides a simplified view of all file system resources across multiple servers and sites, and DFS-R simplifies it further by replicating content between servers. These two combined together form DFS technology in Windows.

 You can read more about this at `http://technet.microsoft.com/en-us/library/jj127250.aspx`.

Both these technologies can be managed to a great extent using PowerShell with the help of the DFS-N and DFS-R modules. The DFS-N module was introduced with Windows Server 2012 and the DFS-R module was introduced with Windows Server 2012 R2. So, you need to have Windows Server 2012 R2 installed to get both the modules. These modules are available and are a part of the DFS Management tools that come with the DFS-N or DFS-R roles installation. If your DFS infrastructure has at least one server with Windows Sever 2012 R2 installed, you can leverage these modules to manage the entire DFS infrastructure. If you don't have a Windows Server 2012 R2 in your DFS infrastructure, you need to write code to query DFS **Windows Management Instrument (WMI)** classes on the Windows Server 2003 and Windows Server 2008 operating systems to manage DFS-N and DSFS-R. Managing DFS through WMI queries is not discussed here and you might want to refer to the MSDN link `http://msdn.microsoft.com/en-us/library/bb540028%28v=vs.85%29.aspx` to understand these WMI classes.

In this chapter, you will be learning about performing the following operations with PowerShell:

- Installing DFS roles
- Managing DFS-N
- Managing DFS-R

Before proceeding further with exploring the usage of these modules, it is important to understand some of the basics of DFS-N so that you will understand the remaining content of this book easily without confusion.

In the following screenshot, you can see two namespaces and we are going to work with one of the namespace called **\\techibee.ad\Personal**:

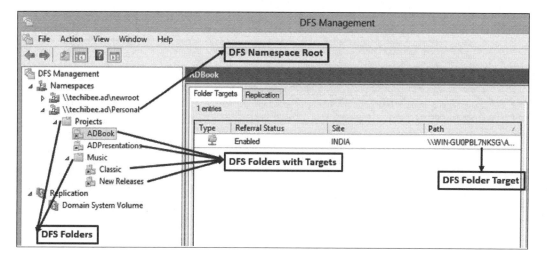

This namespace has a folder inside it with the name **Projects**, that has two folders with links such as **ADBook**, and **ADPresentations** and one folder without any link called **Music**. The **Music** folder has two more folders linked to it, named as **Classic** and **New Releases**.

Here is a brief explanation of DFS-N components that we see in the preceding screenshot:

- **Namespace root**: This is the starting point of the namespace. Since it starts with the name of the domain, it is a domain-based namespace where configuration is stored in Active Directory. The Windows sever that hosts this namespace share is called as namespace server.

- **Namespace folder**: Folders without targets or links are called namespace folders. The purpose of these folders is to form a hierarchy in the namespace. These can have other namespace folders or folders with targets and links as children

- **Namespace folders with targets**: These are the namespace folders that have targets configured. This means that, when you access these folders, they will get redirected to the file shares configured behind them as targets. These targets can be Windows shares, **Network Attached Storage (NAS)** shares, or Samba shares.

Installing DFS roles

The installation process of DFS-N or DFS-R components is very straightforward. These roles can be installed on Windows Server 2008 or later using ServerManager PowerShell module, the default with Windows Server installations. The `Install-WindowsFeature` cmdlet in this module helps to install these roles. These roles can be installed using a GUI as well, but the procedure is not covered here because we want to leverage PowerShell.

Before proceeding with the installation, let's first verify the status of the role. Executing the `Get-WindowsFeature` cmdlet tells us about the role installation status. This cmdlet is also available as part of the ServerManager module.

In the following command, the `FS-DFS-Namespace` and `FS-DFS-Replication` services are the names of the DFS-N and DFS-R roles:

```
PS C:\> Get-WindowsFeature -Name FS-DFS-Replication,FS-DFS-Namespace
  | select DisplayName, Name, Installed | ft -AutoSize


DisplayName       Name               Installed
-----------       ----               ---------

DFS Namespaces    FS-DFS-Namespace      False
DFS Replication   FS-DFS-Replication    False


PS C:\>
```

The **Installed** column specifies whether a role is currently installed or not. If none of these roles are installed, both the roles have a `False` value in the **Installed** column.

Installing the DFS-N role

DFS-N can be installed using the `Install-WindowsFeature` command by passing a FS-DFS-N name to it. Since we are installing DFS components for the first time on this box, let's choose to install DFS Management tools as well by adding the `-IncludeManagementTools` parameter. In the following command, we have used the `-ComputerName` parameter to install the DFS Management tools on the TIBDC3 computer. You can omit this parameter to install the tools on local computer:

```
PS C:\>Install-WindowsFeature -Name FS-DFS-Namespace -
  IncludeManagementTools -ComputerName TIBDC3


Success Restart Needed Exit Code       Feature Result
------- -------------- ---------       --------------
True    No             Success         {DFS NamespacesDFS Management
Tools, Fi...
PS C:\>
```

The preceding output shows that the DFS-N feature (along with the Management tools) is successfully installed and no rebooting is required after installation. You can automate the reboot by adding the `-Restart` switch to the preceding command. Once this has been done, verify the installation of the DFS-N and DFS Management tools by running the following command:

```
Get-WindowsFeature -Name FS-DFS-Namespace, RSAT-DFS-Mgmt-Con -
  ComputerName TIBDC3
```

The output of the preceding command is shown in the following screenshot:

```
PS C:\> Get-WindowsFeature -Name FS-DFS-Namespace, RSAT-DFS-Mgmt-Con -ComputerName TIBDC3

Display Name                              Name                    Install State
------------                              ----                    -------------
    [X] DFS Namespaces                    FS-DFS-Namespace            Installed
        [X] DFS Management Tools          RSAT-DFS-Mgmt-Con           Installed

PS C:\> _
```

Note: The ServerManager module in Windows Server 2008 (with and without R2) didn't support the installation of roles remotely; we did this in the preceding command using the `-ComputerName` parameter. The cmdlets should be executed locally on these server versions for installation of roles. Also, the `Install-WindowsFeature` cmdlet is not available in Windows Server 2008 and you need to use the `Add-WindowsFeature` cmdlet instead.

After the installation, you can verify functionality by opening the DFS Management console.

Installing the DFS-R role

Installation of the DFS-R role is similar to the installation of the DFS-N role. Its just that you need to change role name to DFS-R. Use the following command to do so:

```
Install-WindowsFeature -Name FS-DFS-Replication -
  IncludeManagementTools -ComputerName TIBDC3
```

After running the preceding command successfully, verify the installation status by running the `Get-WindowsFeature` cmdlet:

```
Get-WindowsFeature -Name FS-DFS-Replication, RSAT-DFS-Mgmt-Con
```

You will get an output similar to the one shown in the following screenshot:

```
PS C:\> Get-WindowsFeature -Name FS-DFS-Replication, RSAT-DFS-Mgmt-Con

Display Name                                    Name                      Install State
------------                                    ----                      -------------
    [X] DFS Replication                         FS-DFS-Replication            Installed
        [X] DFS Management Tools                RSAT-DFS-Mgmt-Con             Installed


PS C:\> _
```

As indicated in the preceding output, the DFS-R role is successfully installed along with Management tools.

Managing DFS-N

In this section, you will learn about managing DFS-N using PowerShell. The DFS-N module that we just installed in the previous section comes with a large number of cmdlets for managing DFS-N. Throughout this section, we will make use of some of these cmdlets to perform the management of DFS-N.

You can view all the cmdlets in the DFS-N module using the following command:

```
Get-Command -Module DFSN
```

There are 23 cmdlets in this module that can help in performing various DFS-N operations. We will be using these modules to query, create, modify, and delete namespaces, DFS folders, and targets in following sections. You can refer to the TechNet page at http://technet.microsoft.com/en-us/library/jj884270. aspx to know more about these cmdlets.

Querying DFS namespaces

In this section, you will be learning how to query lists of namespaces in the domain environment and their configuration details. Lists of DFS-N roots in a domain environment can be queried using the Get-DFSNRoot cmdlet, as shown in the following command:

```
Get-DFSNRoot
```

This queries and displays all DFS-N roots in the current domain. If you would like to query DFS-N roots from a different domain, then you can use the -Domain parameter as shown in the following command:

```
Get-DfsnRoot -Domain sales.techibee.ad
```

This queries all the DFS-N roots in the sales.techibee.ad domain.

These queries fetch the data from **Computer Integrated Manufacturing (CIM)** classes in the background. If you want to see what CIM classes are queried, pipe the output to Format-List cmdlet as shown in the following command:

```
Get-DfsnRoot -Domain techibee.ad | Format-List *
```

The CIM * properties in the output show details about the CIM classes. You can read more about CIM classes at the MSDN page at http://msdn.microsoft.com/en-us/library/aa386179%28v=vs.85%29.aspx.

The output of the preceding command is shown in the following screenshot:

```
PS C:\> Get-DfsnRoot -Domain techibee.ad | Format-List *


Path                    : \\techibee.ad\newroot
TimeToLiveSec           : 300
State                   : Online
Flags                   :
Type                    : Domain V2
Description             :
NamespacePath           : \\techibee.ad\newroot
TimeToLive              : 300
GrantAdminAccess        : {techibee\Domain Admins, NT AUTHORITY\SYSTEM, techibee\Enterprise Admins}
PSComputerName          :
CimClass                : ROOT/Microsoft/Windows/DFSN:MSFT_DFSNamespace
CimInstanceProperties   : {Description, Flags, NamespacePath, State...}
CimSystemProperties     : Microsoft.Management.Infrastructure.CimSystemProperties

Path                    : \\techibee.ad\Personal
TimeToLiveSec           : 300
State                   : Online
Flags                   : Site Costing
Type                    : Domain V2
Description             :
NamespacePath           : \\techibee.ad\Personal
TimeToLive              : 300
GrantAdminAccess        : {techibee\Domain Admins, NT AUTHORITY\SYSTEM, techibee\Enterprise Admins}
PSComputerName          :
CimClass                : ROOT/Microsoft/Windows/DFSN:MSFT_DFSNamespace
CimInstanceProperties   : {Description, Flags, NamespacePath, State...}
CimSystemProperties     : Microsoft.Management.Infrastructure.CimSystemProperties


PS C:\>
```

All DFS namespace roots are hosted on a Windows Server. This is called the namespace target. You can view the server on which a DFS-N root is hosted with the help of the following command:

```
Get-DfsnRootTarget -Path \\techibee.ad\Personal | Format-List
```

As you can see in the following screenshot, the `TargetPath` property shows the share name where the DFS-N root details are stored. It also gives additional details such as their status (online/offline) and priority details:

```
PS C:\> Get-DfsnRootTarget -Path \\techibee.ad\Personal | Format-List


Path                    : \\techibee.ad\Personal
TargetPath              : \\WIN-GUOPBL7NKSG\Personal
State                   : Online
ReferralPriorityClass   : sitecost-normal
ReferralPriorityRank    : 0


PS C:\>
```

If your organization has lots of DFS-N root namespaces and you would like to get only the namespaces that match a particular string, you can use the `Where-Object` parameter to filter it, as shown in the following command:

```
Get-DfsnRoot -Domain techibee.ad | Where-Object {$_.Path -match
  "personal" }
```

The following screenshot shows a DFS namespace with names containing the word **personal**, displayed as a result of the filtering we did:

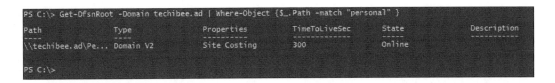

```
PS C:\> Get-DfsnRoot -Domain techibee.ad | Where-Object {$_.Path -match "personal" }
Path               Type        Properties      TimeToLiveSec     State      Description
----               ----        ----------      -------------     -----      -----------
\\techibee.ad\Pe... Domain V2  Site Costing    300               Online

PS C:\>
```

So far, we have discussed querying DFS namespaces that are hosted in domain mode. If you ever attempt to create DFS-N root namespace from the DFS Management GUI, you will notice that DFS-N root namespace can be created as a standalone namespace. In such cases, the namespace root is accessed using the name of the server where the namespace is hosted.

The Get-DFSNRoot cmdlet can be used to query such standalone DFS namespaces as well. To query the details, you need to pass the name of the DFS server to this cmdlet using the -ComputerName parameter, as shown in the following command:

```
Get-DfsnRoot -ComputerName TIBDC2
```

The output should look like the following screenshot:

As you can notice in this output screenshot, the **Type** column indicates what type of DFS-N root namespace it is.

Refer to the MSDN link http://msdn.microsoft.com/en-us/library/ jj152371%28v=vs.85%29.aspx. There are three types of DFS-N root namespaces that can be created. They are as follows:

- Standalone
- Domain V1 (Windows Server 2000 mode)
- Domain V2 (Windows Server 2008 mode)

The feature set of each of these unique, and Domain V2 mode is the best.

This completes querying the DFS namespace details using PowerShell. Now, let's move on to querying DFS-N folders and the targets configured behind them.

Querying DFS-N folders and targets

So far, you have learned how to query the details of DFS-N roots. In this section, we will look at querying folders and targets inside the root namespace. This can be achieved using the Get-DfsnFolder cmdlet as shown in the following command:

```
Get-DfsnFolder -Path \\techibee.ad\Personal\*
```

This lists all the DFS-N folders that have targets. In the following screenshot, the `Format-Table` cmdlet with the `-Autosize` parameter is used to show values of all properties clearly. Otherwise, you will see property values ending with dots. The output here shows the list of DFS folders and their **State (Offline** or **Online)**, together with a few additional configuration details of DFS folders:

```
PS C:\> Get-DfsnFolder -Path \\techibee.ad\Personal\* | ft -AutoSize

Path                                         State  TimeToLiveSec Properties Description
----                                         -----  ------------- ---------- -----------
\\techibee\Personal\Projects\ADPresentations Online 1800
\\techibee\Personal\Projects\Music\New Releases Online 1800
\\techibee\Personal\Projects\Music\Classic   Online 1800
\\techibee\Personal\Projects\ADBook          Online 1800

PS C:\>
```

Note: If there is a folder in the DFS-N structure that has no target set and no child items exists, then you might see a description such as "temporary link used by the DFS UI". Please do not delete that folder.

Each of these folders will have at least one target set and we can access the targets of these folders using the `Get-DFSNFolderTarget` cmdlet, as shown in the following command:

```
Get-DfsnFolderTarget -Path
  \\techibee\Personal\Projects\ADPresentations
```

This command lists all the targets behind this DFS-N folder. These targets are the actual file shares where the data is placed. The following output screenshot shows the DFS-N folders and the targets behind them:

```
PS C:\> Get-DfsnFolderTarget -Path \\techibee\Personal\Projects\ADPresentations | ft -AutoSize

Path                                         TargetPath        State  ReferralPriorityClass ReferralPriorityRank
----                                         ----------        -----  --------------------- --------------------
\\techibee\Personal\Projects\ADPresentations \\WIN-GUOPBL7NK5G\PPTs Online global-high           0
\\techibee\Personal\Projects\ADPresentations \\TIBDC2\PPTs     Online sitecost-normal          0

PS C:\>
```

This output helps you to understand other configuration parameters, for example knowing which one has the highest priority, and so on. As you can see in the preceding screenshot, the first target has the **ReferralPriorityClass** column set to the `global-high` value.

This information is the same as what you see when you go to the DFS tab of the **\\techibee.ad\Personal\Projects\ADPresentations** folder from Windows Explorer, as shown in the following screenshot:

 Note that, if you see a discrepancy between what you see in the PowerShell output and what you see in File Explorer in terms of target lists, then it can be a caching-related issue on the computer where you are using the Explorer. In such cases, run the dfsutil /pktflush command from the command line to clear the local DFS cache and let Explorer get fresh details from the DFS namespace servers. The output you see from PowerShell is more accurate because it fetches the data from DFS namespace servers directly.

You can query all folders and their targets in a given DFS-N root using the following command. It exports the data into Excel for easy viewing and filtering:

```
Get-DfsnFolder -Path \\techibee.ad\Personal\* | % {Get-
    DfsnFolderTarget -Path $_.Path } |Export-csv c:\temp\DFS-N-
    PerSonal.csv -NoTypeInformation
```

The contents of output CSV appear similar to what is shown in the following screenshot:

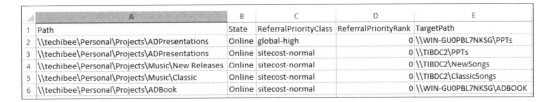

	A	B	C	D	E
1	Path	State	ReferralPriorityClass	ReferralPriorityRank	TargetPath
2	\\techibee\Personal\Projects\ADPresentations	Online	global-high	0	\\WIN-GU0PBL7NKSG\PPTs
3	\\techibee\Personal\Projects\ADPresentations	Online	sitecost-normal	0	\\TIBDC2\PPTs
4	\\techibee\Personal\Projects\Music\New Releases	Online	sitecost-normal	0	\\TIBDC2\NewSongs
5	\\techibee\Personal\Projects\Music\Classic	Online	sitecost-normal	0	\\TIBDC2\ClassicSongs
6	\\techibee\Personal\Projects\ADBook	Online	sitecost-normal	0	\\WIN-GU0PBL7NKSG\ADBOOK

You can explore this topic further by viewing the help content of the `Get-DFSNFolder` and `Get-DFSNFolderTarget` cmdlets.

Creating the DFS-N root and folders

So far, we have seen how to query the existing DFS-N data. This section covers how to create DFS-N root namespaces and folders. The `New-DFSNRoot` and `New-DFSNFolder` cmdlets are used for this purpose.

To create a new DFS-N root, similar to the **\\techibee.ad\personal** folder, we first need to create a share on the DFS namespace server where we want to host this configuration. Say for example, we want to create a new root for the Sales department so that they can access their data through this namespace. We also identified the `TIBDC2` server, which will host this namespace. Then we need to create a share on the `TIBDC2` server with any name of our choice. This share name is used with the `-TargetPath` parameter of the `New-DFSNRoot` cmdlet, as shown in the following command:

```
New-DfsnRoot -Path \\techibee.ad\Sales -TargetPath \\TIBDC2\Sales -
    Type DomainV2
```

As you can see in the preceding command, we have defined the new DFS-N root path as the **\\techibee.ad\sales** folder and the target path is set to the share that we created on the `TIBDC2` server. This DFS-N root is of `DomainV2` type.

Note: It is important to create the target share beforehand. Otherwise, the cmdlet will give reporting errors related to accessing the share. Also, ensure that the domain administrator has full control on this share.

After the preceding command has executed successfully, the new DFS-N root namespace will appear in the **DFS Management** console as shown in the following screenshot. As you can see in the screenshot, the **\\techibee.ad\sales** DFS namespace is listed in the **DFS Management** console:

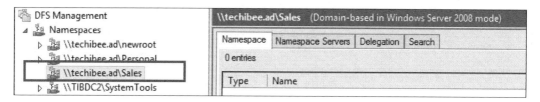

Now that we have a new root setup, let's add some folders to it. The New-DFSNFolder cmdlet helps in doing this, as shown in the following command:

```
New-DfsnFolder -Path \\techibee.ad\Sales\Reports
  \\TIBDC2\SalesReports  -Description "All the reports of sales
  department are here"
```

The preceding sample command is used to create a DFS folder with the target. Depending on the type of DFS-N root, you can set different parameters for the DFS folder during its creation. Some of them are EnableInsiteReferrals, EnableTargetFailback, ReferralPriorityClass, ReferralPriorityRank, state, and so on.

You can view the full help content of the New-DFSNFolder cmdlet to know more about these parameters and their significance by using the following command:

```
Get-Help New-DfsnFolder -Full
```

The next section helps to understand how to add targets to existing DFS-N folders.

Adding and removing folder targets

In the previous section, you learned about creating new DFS-N roots and folders. This section will help you to understand how to add targets to existing DFS-N folders and remove them if necessary.

The cmdlets used for achieving this task are New-DfsnFolderTarget and Remove-DfsnFolderTarget. If you would like to add a new target to the folder we created in the last section, we can do it using the New-DfsnFolderTarget cmdlet. Before proceeding with the command, we need to ensure that the new target is created and accessible.

The following command adds a new target `\\tibdc2\salesreports-backup` to the `\\techibee.ad\sales\Reports` folder. It also sets the priority level to `GlobalHigh` while adding it:

```
New-DfsnFolderTarget -Path \\techibee.ad\sales\Reports -TargetPath
   \\TIBDC2\SalesReports-Backup -ReferralPriorityClass GlobalHigh
```

After the addition, you can view the current targets for the `\\techibee.ad\sales\reports` folder by running the following command:

```
Get-DfsnFolderTarget -Path \\techibee.ad\sales\Reports
```

From the following screenshot, we can see that the new target we added is reflected in the configuration:

You will see the same thing in the **DFS** tab of the **Reports Properties** dialog in the following screenshot:

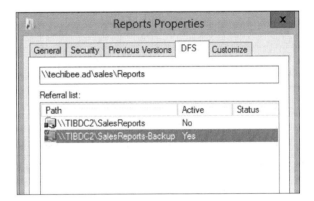

Removing a target path from a DFS folder is also straightforward and we need to use the `Remove-DFSNFolderTarget` cmdlet for this purpose:

```
Remove-DfsnFolderTarget -Path \\techibee.ad\sales\Reports -TargetPath
   \\TIBDC2\SalesReports
```

This will prompt you to confirm the removal of the given target path from the DFS-N folder. This can be suppressed using the `-Confirm:$false` parameter. If you receive errors during the removal, try using the `-Force` switch.

Similarly, the DFS-N folder itself can be removed from the DFS namespace. Removing a DFS-N folder will delete the complete configuration of that folder including the targets. This is shown by the following command:

```
Remove-DfsnFolder -Path \\techibee.ad\sales\Reports
```

This removes the `\\techibee.ad\sales\Reports` folder along with its target entries.

Note: Either deleting the targets or deleting the DFS folder itself will just delete the references to target paths in the DFS configuration. This will not touch any data inside the target paths.

This completes the topic of managing DFS-N using PowerShell and the DFS-N module.

Managing DFS-R

DFS-R is a technology to replicate data between two Windows Servers. You can choose to keep data in the `d:\Project` folder on SERVER1 in sync with the `e:\Project` folder on SERVER2. To do this, you need to have the DFS-R role installed on both the servers. The installation section at the beginning of this chapter will help you with detailed steps to install the DFS-R service and DFS Management tools. The replication can be a two-way replication or one-way replication based on requirements. This is what DFS-R is in a nutshell.

You can visit `http://msdn.microsoft.com/en-us/library/cc771058.aspx` to know more about DFS-R in detail.

As mentioned earlier, Microsoft released a PowerShell module called DFS-R with Windows Server 2012 R2 release. This section completely relies on this module for performing DFS-R related operations. These cmdlets will not work on previous versions of operating system.

The DFS-R module has a total of 42 cmdlets to perform DFS-R related operations. This section focuses on some of the most commonly used cmdlets as they are required during the demonstration. A complete list of cmdlets in this module is available at `http://technet.microsoft.com/en-us/library/dn296591.aspx`.

You can also get this list by running the `Get-Command -Module DFSR` cmdlet.

Before proceeding with querying using PowerShell, let's brush up a little bit on the building blocks of DFS-R. As you can see from the DFS Management console, DFS-R has groups that keep the configuration related to replication of a set of folders.

A DFS-R Group consists of the following information:

- **Member Servers**: These are the servers where DFS-R components are installed and have folders to be replicated.

- **Connections**: These are the objects that define the replication topology between the member servers. If there is a connection from SERVER1 to SERVER2, it means that data is replicating from SERVER1 to SERVER2. Data from SERVER2 to SERVER1 will not get replicated unless there is another connection for it.

- **Replicated Folders**: These define which folders are replicated between the member servers. They contains the path at source and path at destination.

So, for any DFS-R replication to work successfully, we should have these three components configured correctly. All our examples in following DFS-R section revolve around these components only.

Querying DFS-R groups and settings

Let's start exploring the usage of the DFS-R module by starting with querying existing DFS-R groups and configuration. Beginning from Windows Server 2008 R2, the SYSVOL replication started relying on DFS-R for efficient replication. So, if you have SYSVOL replication happening through DFS-R in your environment, you will see the **Domain System Volume** DFS-R Group in the **DFS Management** GUI, as shown in the following screenshot:

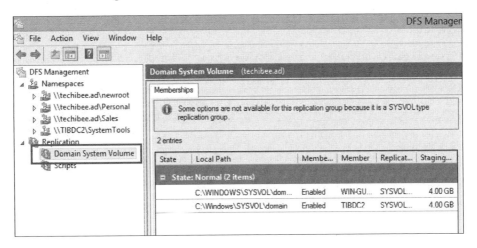

As you can see in the preceding screenshot, there are two DFS-R groups at the moment and one of them is the **Domain System Volume**, which is for SYSVOL replication. We can query the list of DFS-R groups by running the `Get-DFSReplicationGroup` cmdlet, as shown in the following screenshot:

```
PS C:\> Get-DfsReplicationGroup -IncludeSysvol

GroupName    : Domain System Volume
DomainName   : techibee.ad
Identifier   : 3405375b-9e0b-4c7d-8b67-e73c547fda95
Description  :
State        : Normal

GroupName    : Scripts
DomainName   : techibee.ad
Identifier   : ebddc78a-298c-4629-bc41-8f291b323cc2
Description  :
State        : Normal


PS C:\> _
```

As you can see in the output, the `-IncludeSysVol` switch is used with the `Get-DfsReplicationGroup` cmdlet. Without this switch the cmdlet will show only the **Scripts** DFS-R group. The output will also contain information about the group, such as **Identifier**, **DomainName**, **Description**, and **State**. The **State** parameter indicates the current state of the replication group. If the **State** is set to `InComplete`, it means that there is some issue with the replication group configuration.

You can query a single DFS-R group details using the `-GroupName` parameter, as shown in the following command:

```
Get-DfsReplicationGroup -GroupName Scripts
```

Find the members of a replication group using the `Get-DfsrMember` cmdlet, as shown in the following command:

```
Get-DfsReplicationGroup -GroupName Scripts | Get-DfsrMember
```

Running the preceding command will show the `ComputerName`, `Site Name`, and `Connection` details of each DFS-R member that is configured inside the group. This information is the same as what you see in the **Membership** tab of the respective group in the **DFS Management** console.

The members in a DFS-R group communicate with each other based on what is configured in the **Connections** tab in the **DFS Management** console. This information includes Source Server, destination server, Enable status, and other details. These details can be queried using the `Get-DfsrConnection` cmdlet, as shown in the following command:

```
PS C:\> Get-DfsReplicationGroup -GroupName Scripts | Get-
   DfsrConnection


GroupName                  : Scripts
SourceComputerName         : TIBDC2
DestinationComputerName    : WIN-GU0PBL7NKSG
DomainName                 : techibee.ad
Identifier                 : e5106ebe-0457-437f-9e7f-2e8e3a9ea40c
Enabled                    : True
RdcEnabled                 : True
CrossFileRdcEnabled        : True
Description                :
MinimumRDCFileSizeInKB     : 64
State                      : Normal
GroupName                  : Scripts
SourceComputerName         : WIN-GU0PBL7NKSG
DestinationComputerName    : TIBDC2
DomainName                 : techibee.ad
Identifier                 : 6ca2a9f2-c232-4f10-959f-4c2471640472
Enabled                    : True
RdcEnabled                 : True
CrossFileRdcEnabled        : True
Description                :
MinimumRDCFileSizeInKB     : 64
State                      : Normal


PS C:\>
```

This command gives a list of connections, the source, and the destination server of each connection, its Enable status, and other information. This information is the same as what you see in the **Connections** tab of the **Replication** group in the **DFS Management** GUI. This can be seen in the following screenshot:

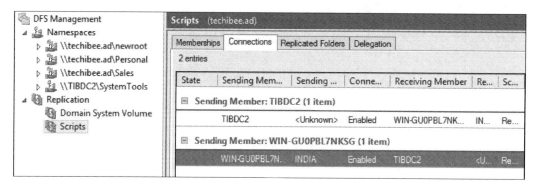

So far, we have seen how to query memberships and connections configured in a replication group. Now, let's verify the actual folders being replicated. Surprisingly, there is no cmdlet in the DFS-R module that can actually query the paths of folders being replicated in the source and destinations. However, we can build our own function using the underlying WMI classes.

Here is one such simple function, that identifies the members of a given replication group and connects to them using WMI to fetch the actual folders being replicated:

```
function Get-ReplicatedFolderPaths {
[cmdletbinding()]
param(
    [string]$FolderName
)

Import-Module Dfsr

$members = Get-DfsReplicatedFolder -FolderName $FolderName | Get-
DfsrMember
foreach($member in $members) {
    $Rgs = Get-WmiObject -Namespace Root\MicrosoftDFS -Class
DfsrReplicatedFolderConfig -ComputerName $member.ComputerName
    $Rgs | ? {$_.ReplicatedFolderName -eq $FolderName } | select
PSComputerName, ReplicatedFolderName, RootPath
}
}
```

Following is the command, that queries the replication partners of the replication group with the name PowerShell and gets the actual folder names being replicated:

```
PS C:\> Get-ReplicatedFolderPaths -FolderName PowerShell | ft -
  AutoSize


PSComputerName    ReplicatedFolderName RootPath
--------------    -------------------- --------

WIN-GU0PBL7NKSG PowerShell              C:\scripts\PowerShell
TIBDC2          PowerShell              C:\Scripts\PowerShell


PS C:\>
```

The output that you see can be found in the **Memberships** tab in the **DFS Management** GUI, as shown in the following screenshot:

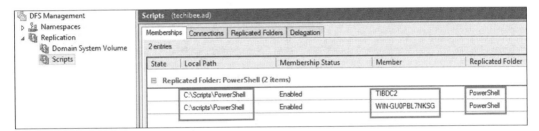

If you want to query any other details that are not available through the DFS-R module, you can leverage DFS-R WMI classes to fetch the information. The following command will help to aquire the list of WMI classes related to DFS-R:

```
Get-WmiObject -Namespace Root\MicrosoftDFS -List | ? {$_.Name -match
  "dfs" }
```

The namespace `Root\MicrosoftDFS` is for V1 version of DFS-R WMI classes. Starting with Windows Server 2012 R2, Microsoft introduced the V2 version of WMI classes, which can be accessed from the `Root\Microsoft\Windows\DFSR` namespace. The V1 namespace is also available in Server 2012 R2 to support the legacy.

Creating a DFS-R group

In the previous section, we have seen how to query existing DFS-R groups and their configuration. Now, let's look at creating a new DFS-R group and configuring it for replicating folders between two servers.

Creating a DFS-R group and configuring it is a step-by-step process. Before you start, ensure that you have actually installed DFS-R roles on member servers where you want to replicate the data. Once roles are installed, we can proceed with DFS-R group creation and configuration.

First, let's create a new DFS-R group called `VBScripts`. The `New-DfsReplicationGroup` cmdlet in the DFS-R module helps in creating a new group, as shown in the following command:

```
PS C:\> New-DfsReplicationGroup -GroupName VBScripts


GroupName    : VBScripts

DomainName   : techibee.ad

Identifier   : b00e9ea4-c38a-4079-af7b-9d7494a8852f

Description  :

State        : Normal


PS C:\>
```

Once the group is created, we need to create a replication folder object and associate it with the newly created group. The `New-DfsReplicatedFolder` cmdlet helps in doing this as shown in the following command:

```
PS C:\> New-DfsReplicatedFolder -GroupName VBScripts -FolderName
  AllVBScripts


GroupName              : VBScripts

FolderName             : AllVBScripts

DomainName             : techibee.ad

Identifier             : 59c80183-996b-4766-b589-a8039f9b274f

Description            :

FileNameToExclude      : {~*, *.bak, *.tmp}

DirectoryNameToExclude : {}

DfsnPath               :
```

```
IsDfsnPathPublished     : False
State                   : Normal
```

PS C:\>

Once the replication folder object is created and associated to the group, let's add the members to the group. Say we have a VBscripts group in the TIBDC2 server at the C:\Scripts\VBScripts path, and we want to replicate them to the C:\Scripts\VBScripts-Backup folder on the TIBDC3 server. So, to achieve this we need to add TIBDC2 and TIBDC3 as members to the VBScripts DFS-R group. It can be done using the Add-DfsrMember cmdlet by passing the replication group name and member names, as shown in the following command:

```
PS C:\> Add-DfsrMember -GroupName VBScripts -ComputerName
  TIBDC2,TIBDC3
```

```
GroupName                        : VBScripts
ComputerName                     : TIBDC2
DomainName                       : techibee.ad
Identifier                       : 533ba2d5-4066-48e4-a4ed-7976dd0aa778
Description                      :
DnsName                          : TIBDC2.techibee.ad
Site                             : INDIA
NumberOfConnections              : 0
NumberOfInboundConnections       : 0
NumberOfOutboundConnections      : 0
NumberOfInterSiteConnections     : 0
NumberOfIntraSiteConnections     : 0
IsClusterNode                    : False
State                            : Normal
GroupName                        : VBScripts
ComputerName                     : TIBDC3
DomainName                       : techibee.ad
Identifier                       : c5662173-c3f4-4fb0-ae3a-73b374620521
Description                      :
DnsName                          : TIBDC3.techibee.ad
Site                             : INDIA
NumberOfConnections              : 0
```

```
NumberOfInboundConnections    : 0

NumberOfOutboundConnections   : 0

NumberOfInterSiteConnections  : 0

NumberOfIntraSiteConnections  : 0

IsClusterNode                 : False

State                         : Normal


PS C:\>
```

After adding members to the group, it will show the properties of each member added. As you can see, TIBDC2 and TIBDC3 are added as members to the VBScripts replication group.

Once added, we need to create connections between them to control the replication. In this case, I want all my scripts in TIBDC2 to be transferred to the TIBDC3 server. This means I want a one-way replication; it can be done using the following command:

```
PS C:\>Add-DfsrConnection -GroupName VBScripts -SourceComputerName TIBDC2
-DestinationComputerName TIBDC3 -CreateOneWay
```

```
GroupName                 : VBScripts

SourceComputerName        : TIBDC2

DestinationComputerName   : TIBDC3

DomainName                : techibee.ad

Identifier                : fad5bec6-fe21-4f66-b4dd-b8fbeaadb111

Enabled                   : True

RdcEnabled                : True

CrossFileRdcEnabled       : True

Description               :

MinimumRDCFileSizeInKB    : 64

State                     : Normal


PS C:\>
```

This created a new connection with the source computer as TIBDC2 and the destination computer as TIBDC3.

Note: We used the `-CreateOneWay` switch with the `Add-DfsrConnection` cmdlet to create the connection. If this is not specified, bidirectional connections will get created between the members.

After the connections are created, we need to tell the members which folders should be replicated. It can be configured using the `Set-DfsrMembership` cmdlet, as shown in the following command:

```
PS C:\> Set-DfsrMembership -GroupName VBScripts -FolderName
  AllVBScripts -ComputerName TIBDC2 -ContentPath
  "C:\Scripts\VBScripts" -PrimaryMember $true -force
```

```
GroupName                    : VBScripts

ComputerName                 : TIBDC2

FolderName                   : AllVBScripts

GroupDomainName              : techibee.ad

ComputerDomainName           : techibee.ad

Identifier                   : 56935cc3-f589-454b-8028-1b708cca990c

DistinguishedName            : CN=59c80183-996b-4766-b589-
a8039f9b274f,CN=07688a05-0c46-4b4d-8fe2-6f41e51e5352,CN=DFSR-L
                               ocalSettings,CN=TIBDC2,OU=Domain
Controllers,DC=techibee,DC=ad

ContentPath                  : C:\Scripts\VBScripts

PrimaryMember                : True

StagingPath                  : C:\Scripts\VBScripts\DfsrPrivate\Staging

StagingPathQuotaInMB         : 4096

MinimumFileStagingSize       : Size256KB

ConflictAndDeletedPath       : C:\Scripts\VBScripts\DfsrPrivate\
ConflictAndDeleted

ConflictAndDeletedQuotaInMB  : 4096

ReadOnly                     : False

RemoveDeletedFiles           : False

Enabled                      : True

DfsnPath                     :

State                        : Normal


PS C:\>
```

After updating the membership for the DFS-R member, it shows the folders that are configured for replication and some other details, that can control the replication. In a similar way, we need to set the membership on the TIBDC3 server as well.

The following command will set the membership details of the VBScript replication group and the AllVBScripts folder:

```
Set-DfsrMembership -GroupName VBScripts -FolderName AllVBScripts -
    ComputerName TIBDC3 -ContentPath "C:\Scripts\VBScripts-Backup" -
    Force
```

> Note: The content path is different from what is configured on TIBDC2. It can be any path on the server that exists. There is no requirement that the source and destination should keep files at the same file-system location.

This completes creating and configuring a new DFS-R replication group. Since the DFS-R settings are stored in Active Directory, it takes some time for the replication to start based on your Active Directory replication schedule and DFS-R refresh frequency. If you want to see things start working immediately, force-replicate the Active Directory to the domain controllers to which these members are connecting and then run the following command:

```
Update-DfsrConfigurationFromAD -ComputerName TIBDC2,TIBDC3
```

This command forces the DFS-R on given computers to read the configuration from Active Directory. Once it is completed, you will see the replication happening.

With this, we have completed the DFS-R replication from the TIBDC2 server to the TIBDC3 server. If you change your mind and now want to configure by directional replication so that changes you make on TIBDC3 contents get replicated to TIBDC2 VBscripts folder, then you can create one more DFS-R connection, as shown in the following command:

```
Add-DfsrConnection -GroupName VBScripts -SourceComputerName TIBDC3 -
    DestinationComputerName TIBDC2 -CreateOneWay
```

After the completion of Active Directory replication, you will see changes replicating in both directions. The configuration of the **VBScripts** replication group appears like the following screenshot from the **DFS Management** GUI:

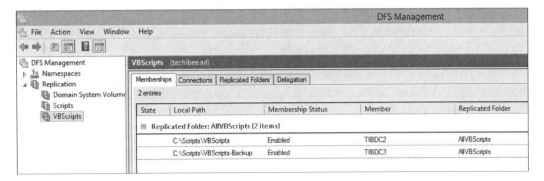

You can explore the help content of these cmdlets further to understand various options for creating replication groups.

Deleting a DFS-R group

Deleting a DFS-R replication group is simple and straightforward. It can be done using the `Remove-DfsReplicationGroup` cmdlet. Deleting the replication group will not cause actual data to be deleted; it just deletes the members, membership details, connections, and other group-related configuration. Using the `-RemoveReplicatedFolders` switch, we are removing all the folder objects that are associated with this group. Use the switch option wisely, as shown in the following command:

```
Remove-DfsReplicationGroup -GroupName VBScripts -
    RemoveReplicatedFolders -Force
```

The preceding command removes the `VBScripts` DFS-R group along with its configuration.

Note: The `-Force` switch is used in the preceding command. It deletes the DFS-R group without asking for confirmation. Remove this switch if you want to review the message and then provide confirmation of deletion.

Summary

In this chapter, you have learned about managing DFS-N and DFS-R using PowerShell. The code samples given are the starting points for getting yourself familiarized with the DFS-N and DFS-R modules. These modules have several cmdlets, each dedicated to perform a particular action. Go through the complete list of cmdlets in these modules to increase your skill.

The next chapter is about managing DNS servers, another core component of Active Directory. They can be managed using the DNSServer module, which comes with the DNS Management tools. You will see how this module comes in handy to perform DNS server and client-related operations.

8
Managing Active Directory DNS Using PowerShell

Domain Naming Service (DNS) is a key component in today's computer world. It plays a crucial role in corporate environments. Without it, logging in to the desktops will not work, all applications may fail to connect to the network, there may be authentication issues everywhere, and even Internet browsing might become impossible. In this chapter, the focus is limited to DNS in the Active Directory environment, Windows client environment, and managing DNS in these areas using PowerShell.

Active Directory relies heavily on DNS to function. Without DNS (Microsoft DNS or Bind), Active Directory cannot function. It uses DNS for various purposes, such as name resolution, the DC locator process, and to identify some of the services in the domain. As a Windows administrator, it is important to understand how to manage DNS in a Windows environment using PowerShell so that most of the daily tasks can be automated and troubleshooting can be done in a faster way.

Microsoft has introduced two DNS-related PowerShell modules with Windows Server 2012. These modules simplify the majority of the DNS administration tasks and help to configure the environment in a much faster way.

The modules are as follows:

1. **DNS server (DNSServer)**: As the name indicates, this module will help in managing DNS server components. Using this module we can create and manage zones, records, servers, configuration, and so on.

2. **DNS client (DNSClient)**: As the name indicates, this is used to manage the DNS Client. This module is handy for identifying and modifying what DNS servers are configured on network adapters, their DNS suffixes, and other information.

There are no significant differences between the DNSServer module in Windows Server 2012 and Windows Server 2012 R2. The only new cmdlet that got added in Windows Server 2012 R2 is the `Step-DnsServerSigningKeyRollover` cmdlet. Also, a few new parameters are added for a couple of cmdlets. The DNS Client module remains the same in both the versions of Windows. You may want to refer to the following article to learn more: `http://technet.microsoft.com/en-us/library/dn305898.aspx`.

In this chapter, we will learn about performing the following tasks using PowerShell:

- Installing and configuring a DNS server
- Working with root hints and forwarders
- Managing DNS zones
- Creating, modifying, and deleting DNS records
- Managing DNS clients

Installing and configuring a DNS server

In this section, let's learn some of the basic Windows DNS server-related operations, installation, and configuration of a DNS server. To start with, how do we know if a given server is a DNS server and can function properly? DNS servers are generally configured on the network adapter in the Windows operating system. If you have multiple network adapters, then it is possible for each adapter to have its own set of DNS servers.

In Windows Server 2012 or later, we can get the DNS server IP addresses that are assigned to local adapters by running the following command:

```
PS C:\> Get-NetIPConfiguration -InterfaceAlias LabNet


InterfaceAlias       : LabNet
InterfaceIndex       : 19
InterfaceDescription : Hyper-V Virtual Ethernet Adapter #3
NetProfile.Name      : techibee.ad
IPv4Address          : 10.10.101.20
IPv4DefaultGateway   :
DNSServer            : 10.10.101.20
                       10.10.101.10
```

This returns the IP configuration details of the network interface with the name `LabNet`. Once we know the DNS server IP addresses, we can perform a test to confirm if they are functioning or not. Also this cmdlet works for Windows Server 2008, and Windows Server 2008 R2. The `Test-DnsServer` cmdlet in the DNSServer module can help in performing this test by using following command:

```
PS C:\> Test-DnsServer -IPAddress 10.10.101.20 | ft -AutoSize


IPAddress      Result   RoundTripTime TcpTried UdpTried
---------      ------   ------------- -------- --------
10.10.101.20 Success 00:00:00      False    True


PS C:\>
```

A "`Success`" message in the output indicates that the IP address passed to the `Test-DnsServer` cmdlet is a valid DNS server and is listening to answer the queries. You will receive a `No Response` message as status if the server is not functional. This cmdlet is also capable of verifying the forwarder functionality and root hints functionality of the DNS server. It can also verify if the given DNS server hosts a zone or not.

As you can see in following screenshot, the `10.10.101.10` DNS server is responding to the normal DNS and the `techibee.ad` zone-based queries, but it is failing when queried for root hints. It is failing because `10.10.101.10` server has no access to the internet so it cannot send queries to root hints:

```
PS C:\> Test-DnsServer -IPAddress 10.10.101.10
IPAddress         Result         RoundTripTime      TcpTried         UdpTried
---------         ------         -------------      --------         --------
10.10.101.10      Success        00:00:11           True             True

PS C:\> Test-DnsServer -IPAddress 10.10.101.10 -ZoneName "techibee.ad"
IPAddress         Result         RoundTripTime      TcpTried         UdpTried
---------         ------         -------------      --------         --------
10.10.101.10      Success        00:00:00           False            True

PS C:\> Test-DnsServer -IPAddress 10.10.101.10 -Context RootHints
IPAddress         Result         RoundTripTime      TcpTried         UdpTried
---------         ------         -------------      --------         --------
10.10.101.10      NoResponse     00:00:12           False            True

PS C:\>
```

Once we have found that the given IP address is a functional DNS server, then we can get further details by using the `Get-DnsServer` cmdlet, as shown in the following command:

```
Get-DnsServer -ComputerName 10.10.101.10
```

This gives a huge amount of detail about the DNS server. The information categories returned by this cmdlet are server settings, serverDsSetting, server scavenging settings, server recursion, server diagnostics, global name zone settings, server cache settings, forwarders, root hints, zones it is hosting, and their aging details. To put it in a simple way, this cmdlet returns all the details that you want to know about the DNS server. Since the output returned by this cmdlet is extensive, this cmdlet provides a few cmdlets that helps in querying the information about each of the aforementioned components. To get these cmdlet names, use the following command:

```
PS C:\> Get-Command -Module DNSServer -Name Get-Dnsserver*
```

CommandType	Name	ModuleName
Function	Get-DnsServer	DNSServer
Function	Get-DnsServerCache	DNSServer
Function	Get-DnsServerDiagnostics	DNSServer
Function	Get-DnsServerDirectoryPartition	DNSServer
Function	Get-DnsServerDnsSecZoneSetting	DNSServer
Function	Get-DnsServerDsSetting	DNSServer
Function	Get-DnsServerEDns	DNSServer
Function	Get-DnsServerForwarder	DNSServer
Function	Get-DnsServerGlobalNameZone	DNSServer
Function	Get-DnsServerGlobalQueryBlockList	DNSServer
Function	Get-DnsServerRecursion	DNSServer
Function	Get-DnsServerResourceRecord	DNSServer
Function	Get-DnsServerRootHint	DNSServer
Function	Get-DnsServerScavenging	DNSServer
Function	Get-DnsServerSetting	DNSServer
Function	Get-DnsServerSigningKey	DNSServer
Function	Get-DnsServerStatistics	DNSServer
Function	Get-DnsServerTrustAnchor	DNSServer
Function	Get-DnsServerTrustPoint	DNSServer
Function	Get-DnsServerZone	DNSServer
Function	Get-DnsServerZoneAging	DNSServer
Function	Get-DnsServerZoneDelegation	DNSServer

```
PS C:\>
```

As you notice in the output, the names of the cmdlets are very intuitive, as they tell you what information they return. Since it is very easy to understand their functionality by looking at the name, further details about each cmdlet individually are not given here. You may get the help content of each cmdlet by using the following command to read more about them. These cmdlets will be used as required throughout this chapter whenever we have a need to query this information:

```
Get-Help <Cmdlet Name> -Full
```

Now that we understand how to query the details of a DNS server, let's proceed with installing a DNS server using PowerShell.

Installing a DNS server

In an Active Directory environment, a DNS server is installed along with domain controller installation. Each DC is expected to have a local DNS server but it is not mandatory; it is a best practice. In *Chapter 6, Advanced AD Operations Using PowerShell*, we learned how to install a DNS server at the time of installing a new domain or domain controller. Now let's see how to install a standalone DNS server. We may or may not use this DNS for hosting Active Directory-integrated zones.

Installation of DNS server components is as good as installing the DNS server feature. This feature can be installed locally or from a remote machine using the `Add-WindowsFeature` cmdlet in the ServerManager module. We can verify the installation status of the DNS role on a remote computer by using the following command:

```
PS C:\> Get-WindowsFeature -Name *dns* -ComputerName TIBSRV4 | select
   DisplayName, Installed | ft -AutoSize


DisplayName       Installed
-----------       ---------
DNS Server        False
DNS Server Tools  False


PS C:\>
```

As you can see in the output, the DNS server role as well as the Management tools are not installed at the moment. Let's proceed to install them. Installation of any role or feature can be performed using the `Add-WindowsFeature` cmdlet. Use the following command to install DNS server and Management tools:

```
PS C:\> Add-WindowsFeature -Name DNS, RSAT-DNS-Server -ComputerName
  TIBSRV4 -IncludeAllSubFeature


Success Restart Needed Exit Code      Feature Result
------- -------------- ---------      --------------

True    No             Success        {DNS Server, Remote Server
Administration


PS C:\>
```

The output of the command shows that the installation was successful, and no restart is needed after installation. If the `Restart Needed` property is `Yes`, then you need to restart the server to complete the installation. The restart can also be automated by using the `-Restart` switch with the preceding command, which will trigger the reboot if a restart is needed to complete the installation.

After the installation, the functionality can be verified using the `Test-DnsServer` command, as shown in the following command:

```
PS C:\> Test-DnsServer -IPAddress 10.10.101.26 | ft -AutoSize


IPAddress     Result  RoundTripTime TcpTried UdpTried
---------     ------  ------------- -------- --------

10.10.101.26 Success 00:00:11       True     True


PS C:\>
```

> The `Test-DnsServer` cmdlet has the `-ComputerName` parameter, which can take the FQDN or NetBIOS name of the server to test for DNS functionality. But even after specifying the parameter, the cmdlet can keep on prompting for the IP address since it is a mandatory property. Because of this the, IP address is passed to the `Test-DnsServer` cmdlet wherever it is used in this book.

This completes the installation of DNS server using PowerShell.

Configuring the DNS server

In this section let's look at some of the common DNS configuration tasks that you need to perform after a new DNS server installation. The configuration of the DNS server depends on an individual organizations needs and customizations.

Changing the listening IP address

When a new DNS server is installed, it listens on all available IP addresses by default. In some cases, the system administrators want to restrict the DNS server to listen on only a particular IP. Let's see how we can achieve this using PowerShell.

If you use DNS Management GUI, you will notice the list of IP addresses the DNS server is listening. You can get this from DNS server properties in the Management console, as shown in the following screenshot:

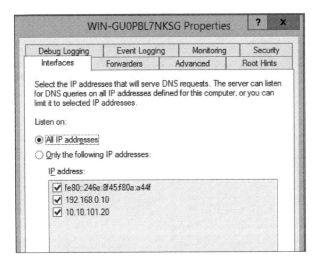

This configuration can be obtained either using the `Get-DnsServer` cmdlet or `Get-DnsServerSetting` cmdlet. Let's explore and see how we can get this information by using following command:

```
Get-DnsServerSetting -All -ComputerName WIN-GU0PBL7NKSG
```

This command returns all settings of the DNS server running on the WIN-GU0PBL7NKSG server. The list of settings returned by this cmdlet is the same as what you see under the `ServerSettings` section of the `Get-DnsServer` cmdlet. The `Get-DnsServerSetting` cmdlet also returns 71 properties that talk about various DNS server configuration settings. If you are just interested in seeing basic components, then you can remove the `-All` switch, as shown in the following command:

```
PS C:\> Get-DnsServerSetting -ComputerName WIN-GU0PBL7NKSG
```

```
ComputerName         : WIN-GU0PBL7NKSG.techibee.ad
MajorVersion         : 6
MinorVersion         : 2
BuildNumber          : 9200
IsReadOnlyDC         : False
EnableDnsSec         : True
EnableIPv6           : True
ListeningIPAddress   : {fe80::246e:8f45:f80a:a44f, 192.168.0.10,
   10.10.101.20}
AllIPAddress         : {fe80::246e:8f45:f80a:a44f, 192.168.0.10,
   10.10.101.20}
```

```
PS C:\>
```

As you can see in the preceding output, the DNS server is listening on all available IP addresses (one IPv6 IP and two IPv4 IPs). If you want to configure the DNS server to listen on only one IP address (for example: 10.10.101.20), then you can use the following commands:

```
$DNSObj = Get-DnsServerSetting -ComputerName WIN-GU0PBL7NKSG -All
$DNSObj.ListeningIPAddress = @("10.10.101.20")
Set-DnsServerSetting -InputObject $DNSObj
```

Using the above commands, first we query the instance of DNS server and store it in the $DNSObj variable. Then we update the `ListeningIPAddress` property of the instance to use the IP that we want to set, and then pass the instance object to the `Set-DnsServerSetting` cmdlet with `-InputObject` parameter so that it can write the changes to the DNS server.

After this change, you can verify the DNS server settings again to verify if the change is applied or not. In the following output, you can see that the ListeningIPAddresses property is updated to use the 10.10.101.20 IP address by using the following command:

```
PS C:\> Get-DnsServerSetting -ComputerName WIN-GU0PBL7NKSG


ComputerName        : WIN-GU0PBL7NKSG.techibee.ad

MajorVersion        : 6

MinorVersion        : 2

BuildNumber         : 9200

IsReadOnlyDC        : False

EnableDnsSec        : True

EnableIPv6          : True

ListeningIPAddress  : 10.10.101.20

AllIPAddress        : {fe80::246e:8f45:f80a:a44f, 192.168.0.10,
   10.10.101.20}


PS C:\>
```

> One thing to note here is that, while creating an instance of the DNS server, the -All switch parameter is used with the Get-DnsServerSetting cmdlet. This is mandatory because the Set-DnsServerSetting cmdlet takes the object type generated with the -All switch. Otherwise, it will fail with errors indicating an incorrect input object type.

You can follow the same approach for changing any property that you see in the Get-DnsServerSetting cmdlet output.

Enabling or disabling recursion

Recursion is another setting that a lot of organizations customize. By default, the DNS server performs recursive queries on behalf of the client and sends back the final reply to it by forwarding the queries to other DNS servers or root hints. It is a name-resolution technique in which the DNS server, queries other DNS servers on behalf of client to deliver the fully resolved name.

We can use the Set-DnsServerRecursion cmdlet to disable or enable recursion on a DNS server as shown in the following command:

```
Set-DnsServerRecursion -ComputerName TIBDC2 -Enable $false
```

This command disables the recursion feature on the TIBDC2 server. So, from now onwards, the TIBDC2 server will answer the queries related to the zones for which it is authorized. For other zones, it will either redirect to a forwarder or root hints.

The current settings of recursion can be viewed by using the Get-DnsServerRecursion cmdlet, as shown in the following command:

```
PS C:\> Get-DnsServerRecursion -ComputerName TIBDC2


Enable              : False
AdditionalTimeout(s) : 4
RetryInterval(s)    : 3
Timeout(s)          : 8
SecureResponse      : True


PS C:\>
```

As you can see in the output, recursion is disabled on the server.

Working with root hints and forwarders

In this section we will focus on how to configure root hints and forwarders for the DNS server that we have just installed. Before proceeding with that, let's learn a bit about root hints and forwarders. They are as follows:

- **Root hints**: Each DNS server is authorized to provide responses to zones hosted on them. But what if the DNS server you are querying is not responsible for the DNS data you are looking for? In such cases, DNS uses the root hint servers to find the authoritative name servers for the domain you are looking for and provides you the results by contacting them. The DNS server should be able to talk to these root hint servers. The default root hint servers are placed on the Internet since your DNS server should have access to these root hints for resolution.

- **Forwarders**: Using root hints for non-authoritative name resolution operations is not always possible. DNS servers in corporate environment may not be allowed to talk to root hint servers on the Internet. In such cases, you can design one or two DNS servers in the corporate environment to communicate with root hints for non-authoritative queries, and the remaining DNS servers can forward the non-authoritative queries to these designed DNS servers. This is done by configuring forwarders in DNS configuration.

The **Internet Assigned Numbers Authority (IANA)** maintains a list of root hint servers for Internet name resolutions and the list is available at `https://www.iana.org/domains/root/files`. You can visit this website if you want more information about root hints. You can also visit `http://www.root-servers.org/` to know the locations of different root hint servers across the globe.

We can query the root hints configured in a Windows DNS server using the `Get-DnsServerRootHint` cmdlet. Using this cmdlet, we can query the root hints of any local or any other Microsoft DNS server in the network, as shown in the following command:

```
PS C:\> Get-DnsServerRootHint -ComputerName TIBDC2


NameServer                          IPAddress
----------                          ---------
b.root-servers.net.                 2001:500:84::b
f.root-servers.net.                 2001:500:2f::f
c.root-servers.net.                 2001:500:2::c
e.root-servers.net.                 192.203.230.10
h.root-servers.net.                 128.63.2.53
g.root-servers.net.                 192.112.36.4
a.root-servers.net.                 2001:503:ba3e::2:30
d.root-servers.net.                 2001:500:2d::d


PS C:\>
```

If you want to add a new root to the list, you can use the `Add-DnsServerRoothint` cmdlet. In the following example, we are adding a new root hint `m.root-servers.net` server to the list and then verifying whether it is added or not by using the `Get-DnsServerRootHint` cmdlet, as shown in the following commands:

```
PS C:\> Add-DnsServerRootHint -ComputerName TIBDC2 -NameServer
   m.root-servers.net. -IPAddress 202.12.27.33 -PassThru


NameServer                                    IPAddress

- - - - - - - - - -                           - - - - - - - - -

m.root-servers.net.                           202.12.27.33


PS C:\> Get-DnsServerRootHint -ComputerName TIBDC2


NameServer                                    IPAddress

- - - - - - - - - -                           - - - - - - - - -

b.root-servers.net.                           2001:500:84::b

f.root-servers.net.                           2001:500:2f::f

c.root-servers.net.                           2001:500:2::c

e.root-servers.net.                           192.203.230.10

h.root-servers.net.                           128.63.2.53

g.root-servers.net.                           192.112.36.4

a.root-servers.net.                           2001:503:ba3e::2:30

d.root-servers.net.                           2001:500:2d::d

m.root-servers.net.                           202.12.27.33


PS C:\>
```

You can see in the preceding output that the `m.root-servers.net` server is added to the list of root hints. Similarly, you can add any list of root hints.

Let's look at another example where you have a server set with the correct list of root hints and then want to replicate it to other DNS servers in your network. There are two ways to achieve that. One way is to, read a list of root hints from the server and add them one by one to the other server you need. Alternatively, you can use the `Import-DnsServerRootHint` cmdlet, which can import the list of root hints in one go. The following code sample demonstrates the second approach. In this example, we are reading the root hints list from the `TIBSRV4` server and applying it to the `TIBDC2` DNS server.

The code, with its description, is as follows:

```
#Import DNS Server module
Import-Module DNSServer

#Read existing root hints in TIBDC2
$RootHints = Get-DnsServerRootHint -ComputerName TIBDC2

#Remove the existing root hits from TIBDC2
foreach($Root in $RootHints) {
    Remove-DnsServerRootHint -ComputerName TIBDC2 -InputObject $Root
-Force
}

#import root hints from TIBSRV4 DNS Server to TIBDC2
Import-DnsServerRootHint -NameServer TIBSRV4 -ComputerName TIBDC2
```

You can see in the preceding code that, we first remove the existing DNS root hints from the server where we want to set the new list. This is because the `Import-DnsServerRootHint` cmdlet appends the list from the source name server to the target. It will not overwrite the existing ones unless there is a conflict in name. That is the reason that we first we remove the existing entries and then import from the source server.

So far we have seen how to manage the root hint servers in DNS server, now let's look at managing forwarders. The DNSServer PowerShell module has a set of cmdlets that can help in adding and removing forwarders (and conditional forwarders) in Microsoft DNS environment. To see the list of cmdlets that help in doing these operations, use the following command:

```
PS C:\> Get-Command -Module DNSServer -Name *Forwarder*


CommandType        Name                                         ModuleName
-----------        ----                                         ----------
Function           Add-DnsServerConditionalForwarderZone        DnsServer
Function           Add-DnsServerForwarder                       DnsServer
Function           Get-DnsServerForwarder                       DnsServer
Function           Remove-DnsServerForwarder                    DnsServer
Function           Set-DnsServerConditionalForwarderZone        DnsServer
Function           Set-DnsServerForwarder                       DnsServer


PS C:\>
```

In the preceding output, the names of the cmdlets are meaningful, and you can easily pick up the cmdlet for a given task. By default, the Microsoft DNS server is configured to use root hints for answering non-authoritative queries. However, the system administrator can configure forwarders so that any queries that cannot be answered by the DNS server will get the forwarded to forwarder of the DNS server for resolution. Forwarders will take precedence over the root hints, and the root hints will be used only when no forwarders are available or are not responding.

Let's first query the configured forwarders in a DNS server by using the following command:

```
PS C:\> Get-DnsServerForwarder -ComputerName TIBSRV4


UseRootHint         : True
Timeout(s)          : 3
EnableReordering    : True
IPAddress           : 10.10.101.20
ReorderedIPAddress  : 10.10.101.20


PS C:\>
```

This command queries the forwarders configured on the TIBSRV4 DNS server. A new forwarder can be added to the list by the Add-DnsServerForwarder cmdlet. It takes the IP address that you want to add as forwarder and the ComputerName server where you want to set this forwarder as shown in the following command:

```
Add-DnsServerForwarder -IPAddress 10.10.101.10 -ComputerName TIBSRV4
```

You can run the Get-DnsServerForwarder cmdlet again to verify if the forwarder is added or not. In the similar way, forwarders can be deleted using the Remove-DnsServerForwarder cmdlet. It takes the same set of parameters that the Add-DnsServerForwarder cmdlet accepts, as shown in the following command:

```
Remove-DnsServerForwarder -IPAddress 10.10.101.20 -ComputerName
   TIBSRV4 -Force
```

The preceding command removes the 10.10.101.20 IP address from the forwarders list. Managing forwarders in a DNS environment is made easy and simple with these cmdlets.

Conditional forwarders

Now let's see how to configure conditional forwarders in DNS. As the name indicates, these forwarders are used for routing the DNS query traffic based on a certain condition (domain name). For example, any queries for the records in `techibee.com` can be forwarded to a specific DNS server instead of using regular forwarders or root hints. This is often used in multi-forest environments to route the DNS traffic from one forest to another.

One limitation of the Microsoft DNSServer module is that it doesn't have a cmdlet to query the existing conditional forwarders from a given DNS server. But don't worry. We can build our own function to get the conditional forwarder details. All these DNS cmdlets makes use of WMI/CIM classes in `Root\MicrosoftDNS` namespace. So for the conditional forwarder details, we can directly query these classes.

The following is a small function wrapped on top of the `MicrosoftDNS_Zone` WMI class that stores zone information. This function can be used to query conditional forwarder details from any DNS server:

```
function Get-DNSConditionalForwarder {
[cmdletbinding()]
param(
    [string]$ComputerName
)
$Zones = @(Get-WmiObject -Class MicrosoftDNS_Zone -Namespace
  Root\MicrosoftDNS -ComputerName $ComputerName | ? {$_.ZoneType -
  eq 4 })

foreach($zone in $Zones) {
  if($Zones) {
    $OutputObj = New-Object -TypeName PSobject
    $OutputObj | Add-Member -MemberType NoteProperty -Name
    DNSServer -Value $ComputerName
    $OutputObj | Add-Member -MemberType NoteProperty -Name
    ZoneName -Value $Zone.Name
    $OutputObj | Add-Member -MemberType NoteProperty -Name
    ForwarderIP -Value $Zone.MasterServers
    $OutputObj
  } else {
    Write-Warning "$ComputerName doesn't have any conditional
    forwarders"
  }
}
}
```

Using this function is very simple. Just copy and paste the code into a PowerShell window and call the function, as shown in the following command:

```
PS C:\> Get-DNSConditionalForwarder -ComputerName TIBSRV4 | ft -AutoSize


DNSServer ZoneName          ForwarderIP
--------- --------          -----------
TIBSRV4   sales.techibee.ad {10.10.101.25}


PS C:\>
```

The TIBSRV4 DNS server has a conditional forwarder for the sales.techibee.ad domain to forward all related queries to the 10.10.101.25 IP address.

We can create a new forwarder zone by using the Add-DnsServerConditionalForw arderZone cmdlet, which takes the name of the domain for which you want to create conditional forwarding and the target DNS server for that domain, as shown in the following command:

```
PS C:\> Add-DnsServerConditionalForwarderZone -ComputerName TIBSRV4 -
  Name google.com -MasterServers 216.239.32.10 -PassThru | ft -
  AutoSize


ZoneName   ZoneType  IsAutoCreated IsDsIntegrated IsReverseLookupZone
IsSigned
--------   --------  ------------- -------------- -------------------  ---
-----
google.com Forwarder False         False          False


PS C:\>
```

Once this is done, you can verify the current conditional forwarders by using the Get-DNSConditionalForwarder function that we just wrote and imported. By default, the Add-DnsServerConditionalForwarderZone cmdlet creates a standalone forwarder zone, which means that the created forwarder configuration is specific to the DNS server. At the time of creation of the forwarding, you can set it as an AD integrated zone by using the -ReplicationScope parameter. When the conditional forwarder zone is created as an AD integrated zone, it will get replicated to other DNS servers based on the scope (domain or forest).

The Set-DnsServerConditionalForwarderZone cmdlet can be used to modify the existing conditional forwarder zones. See its help content for more details.

Managing DNS zones

In the previous sections, we have seen some of the DNS configuration items. In this section, we will find out how to manage zones in a DNS environment. Zones are the actual entities in a DNS environment that store the DNS records and control replication. There are different types of zone available in DNS, each serving a specific purpose.

There are three main types of zone available in DNS. They are as follows:

1. **Primary zone**: As the name indicates, this is the primary source of information for the zone. When a zone is created as primary zone, it can be as a standalone or AD DS-integrated. The standard zone stores the data in file format in the `%windir%\System32\Dns` folder on the DNS server where it is hosted. In the case of AD DS-integrated zone, information is stored in Active Directory based on the replication type set for the zone (domain or forest).

2. **Secondary zone**: This zone acts as backup for a primary zone. It obtains data from the DNS server that hosts the primary zone. The secondary zone stores the data in file format at the `%windir%\System32\Dns` folder on the DNS server where it is hosted.

3. **Stub zone**: When a zone is created as a stub zone, it is only responsible for storing authoritative name servers of the zone it is hosting. It gets this data from DNS servers that actually host the primary zone of the domain.

Though DNSServer module has cmdlets for managing each of these zones, this section focuses only on primary zones. Managing secondary zones and stub zones is similar to managing primary zones, with a slight change based on the functionality. You can read more about these zones at `http://technet.microsoft.com/en-us/library/cc771898.aspx`.

The cmdlets that are useful for managing primary zones can be obtained by using the following command:

```
PS C:\> Get-Command -Module DNSServer -Name *PrimaryZone*
```

CommandType	Name	ModuleName
Function	Add-DnsServerPrimaryZone	DnsServer
Function	ConvertTo-DnsServerPrimaryZone	DnsServer
Function	Restore-DnsServerPrimaryZone	DnsServer
Function	Set-DnsServerPrimaryZone	DnsServer

```
PS C:\>
```

As mentioned before, primary zones can be created as either file-based or AD DS-integrated. In the former, the zone data is stored in a file, and in the latter case, the zone data is stored in Active Directory. The advantage of storing the data in Active Directory is that zone information is replicated along with Active Directory data replication, and no explicit DNS replication is required for transferring the zone to other DNS servers. In the Active Directory-integrated zone, all DNS servers that load the zone information from Active Directory host that zone. Also, all the DNS servers hosting the zone can make modifications to it. But, in the file-based primary zone, a system administrator needs to configure the secondary zone for backup on a different DNS server and ensure that DNS replication is always working.

First let's start with querying existing zones in a DNS server. The Get-DnsServerZone cmdlet can be used to query the available zones on a DNS server as shown in the following command:

```
Get-DNSServerZone -ComputerName TIBDC2 | ft -AutoSize
```

The **IsDsIntegrated** column in the following output screenshot specifies whether it is a file-based zone or AD integrated:

```
PS C:\> Get-DnsServerZone -ComputerName TIBDC2 | ft -AutoSize

ZoneName                ZoneType IsAutoCreated IsDsIntegrated IsReverseLookupZone IsSigned
--------                -------- ------------- -------------- ------------------- --------
_msdcs.techibee.ad      Primary  False         True           False               False
0.in-addr.arpa          Primary  True          False          True                False
101.10.10.in-addr.arpa  Primary  False         True           True                False
127.in-addr.arpa        Primary  True          False          True                False
255.in-addr.arpa        Primary  True          False          True                False
child1.techibee.ad      Primary  False         False          False               False
techibee.ad             Primary  False         True           False               False
TrustAnchors            Primary  False         True           False               False

PS C:\>
```

A true value indicates that it is AD-integrated, otherwise it is file-based. You might have noticed one more property in the output, which says **IsReverseLookupzone**. This indicates whether a zone is forward zone (name-to-IP resolution) or reverse zone (IP-to-name resolution).

Now let's create a new primary forward zone that is standalone by using the following command:

```
Add-DnsServerPrimaryZone -ComputerName TIBDC2 -Name
  child2.techibee.ad -ZoneFile child2.techibee.ad.dns
```

This creates a primary zone with its data stored in the `child2.techibee.ad.dns` file on the `TIBDC2` server. We can verify if the file is created or not using the `Get-ChildItem` PowerShell cmdlet, as shown in the following command:

```
PS C:\> Get-ChildItem '\\tibdc2\c$\windows\system32\dns'


    Directory: \\tibdc2\c$\windows\system32\dns


Mode                LastWriteTime         Length Name
----                -------------         ------ ----
d----         22/10/2014    1:59 AM               backup
d----         23/8/2014    12:06 AM               samples
-a---         23/8/2014    12:07 AM          1171 cache.dns
-a---         23/10/2014   12:33 AM           566 child1.techibee.ad.dns
-a---         23/10/2014   12:43 AM           562 child2.techibee.ad
-a---         23/10/2014   12:44 AM           566 child2.techibee.ad.dns
-a---         22/10/2014    1:59 AM             0 dns.log


PS C:\>
```

Once the zone is created, it is ready for hosting the records. To get complete details about the zone you use the following command:

```
Get-DnsServerZone -ComputerName TIBDC2 -Name child2.techibee.ad | fl
    *
```

After managing it for some time, if you decide to convert this to an Active Directory-integrated zone so that AD replication takes care of replicating it to other DNS servers in the domain or forest, you can convert this zone to AD DS-integrated by using the following command:

```
ConvertTo-DnsServerPrimaryZone -ComputerName TIBDC2 -Name
    child2.techibee.ad -ReplicationScope Domain -Force
```

Once it is converted to AD DS-integrated zone, wait for the replication to complete and then you will start noticing this zone in other AD DNS servers in the same domain. You can also verify this by connecting to the **DC=DomainDNSZones,DC=techibee,DC=AD** naming context. In case you have selected `-ReplicationScope` as forest in previous command, you need to look under the `DC=ForestDNSZones,DC=techibee,DC=ad` naming context. You will find all AD DS-integrated zones under the Microsoft DNS container as shown in the following screenshot:

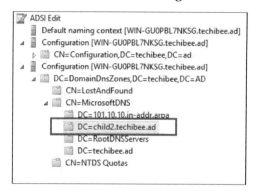

We can make changes to any primary zone by using the `Set-DnsServerPrimayZone` cmdlet. At the time of creating the `child2.techibee.ad` zone, we haven't selected any input for dynamic updates. After converting it to Active Directory-integrated zone, if you want to enable secure dynamic updates on this zone, it can be done using the following command:

```
Set-DnsServerPrimaryZone -Name child2.techibee.ad -ComputerName WIN-
    GU0PBL7NKSG -DynamicUpdate secure
```

In the preceding command you might have noticed that the `WIN-GU0PBL7NKSG` server is used to make changes to the `child2.techibee.ad` zone. Since it is an AD-integrated zone, it doesn't matter on which DNS server we make the change, as it will automatically get replicated to others as per the AD replication schedule. After running the following command, you can verify the details about dynamic updates:

```
PS C:\> Get-DnsServerzone -Name child2.techibee.ad | select ZoneName,
    dynamicupdate,IsDSIntegrated | fl


ZoneName        : child2.techibee.ad
dynamicupdate   : Secure
IsDSIntegrated : True


PS C:\>
```

With this we will conclude this section and start working with DNS records in the next sections.

Creating, modifying, and deleting DNS records

DNS is all about records. It maintains a record name to respective data-type mapping. Following are the frequently used resource record types in DNS:

Record Type	Record Name	Description
A	Address record	Used for mapping a name to IPv4 address.
CNAME	Alias record	Used for mapping an alias to hostname.
NS	Name Server record	Gives details about name servers for a given domain.
PTR	Pointer (or Reverse) record	Maps IP address to a hostname.
SOA	State Of Authority	This contains administrative information about a domain hosted by the zone. Details like who owns it, email ID, refresh interval, retry interval, etc. related to the zone.
MX	Mail Exchange record	This gives the list of email servers that can accept emails for a given domain.
SRV	Service record	This is used for mapping a service to hostname and port details.

There are some more resource record types in DNS that can be created and modified as well, and that serve different data needs. However, they are less common and hence not mentioned in the preceding table. You can refer to `http://technet.microsoft.com/en-us/library/cc958958.aspx` for the full list of resource records supported by Microsoft DNS.

This section focuses on managing A, CNAME, PTR, and SRV records to demonstrate the DNSServer PowerShell module usage. These are the cmdlets that can work with resource records in DNS when using the following command:

```
PS C:\> Get-Command -Module DnsServer -Name *ResourceRecord*
```

CommandType	Name	ModuleName
-----------	----	----------
Function	Add-DnsServerResourceRecord	DnsServer
Function	Add-DnsServerResourceRecordA	DnsServer
Function	Add-DnsServerResourceRecordAAAA	DnsServer
Function	Add-DnsServerResourceRecordCName	DnsServer

Function	Add-DnsServerResourceRecordDnsKey	DnsServer
Function	Add-DnsServerResourceRecordDS	DnsServer
Function	Add-DnsServerResourceRecordMX	DnsServer
Function	Add-DnsServerResourceRecordPtr	DnsServer
Function	Get-DnsServerResourceRecord	DnsServer
Function	Import-DnsServerResourceRecordDS	DnsServer
Function	Remove-DnsServerResourceRecord	DnsServer
Function	Set-DnsServerResourceRecord	DnsServer
Function	Set-DnsServerResourceRecordAging	DnsServer

```
PS C:\>
```

Managing A records and PTR records

When you ping `google.com`, your DNS Client contacts the DNS server for the resource record of type A to give the IP address of `google.com`. From then on, your system communicates with `google.com` using that IP address.

We can query all A records in a domain by using the following command:

```
Get-DnsServerResourceRecord -RRType A -ZoneName techibee.ad
```

The output will contain the **HostName** and **RecordData** columns that contain the name of the host and its IP address that is registered in DNS.

For example, we can query the IP address of `TIBDC2` computer by using the following command:

```
PS C:\> Get-DnsServerResourceRecord -RRType A -ZoneName techibee.ad -
  Name TIBDC2   | ft -AutoSize


HostName RecordType Timestamp TimeToLive RecordData
-------- ---------- --------- ---------- ----------
TIBDC2   A          0         01:00:00   10.10.101.10


PS C:\>
```

As you can see in the output, the `10.10.101.10` IP address is mapped to the `TIBDC2` server.

A new A type resource record can be created in a zone using either the Add-DnsServerResourceRecord cmdlet or Add-DnsServerResourceRecordA cmdlet, as shown in the following command:

```
Add-DnsServerResourceRecord -A -ZoneName techibee.ad -ComputerName
    TIBDC2 -Name testpc20 -IPv4Address 10.10.101.30
```

The Add-DnsServerResourceRecord cmdlet has several options to create resource records. If you feel this cmdlet is confusing to understand because of its number of options, then you can switch to the respective resource record creation cmdlet (for example, Add-DnsServerResourceRecordA to create an A type resource record).

You can verify that the record is created by using the following command:

```
PS C:\> Get-DnsServerResourceRecord -Name testpc20 -ComputerName
    TIBDC2 -RRType A  -ZoneName techibee.ad | fl


DistinguishedName : DC=testpc20,DC=techibee.ad,cn=MicrosoftDNS,
    DC=DomainDnsZones,DC=techibee,DC=ad

HostName          : testpc20

RecordType        : A

RecordClass       : IN

TimeToLive        : 01:00:00

Timestamp         : 0

RecordData        : 10.10.101.30


PS C:\>
```

The Resolve-DNSName cmdlet in the DNS Client module is used for testing the resolution status of a record. Let's try it and see if it is able to resolve our newly created DNS A record, as shown in the following command:

```
PS C:\> Resolve-DnsName -Name testpc20 -Server TIBDC2 | fl


Name       : testpc20.techibee.ad

Type       : A

TTL        : 3600

DataLength : 4

Section    : Answer

IPAddress  : 10.10.101.30


PS C:\>
```

It is able to resolve the `testpc20.techibee.ad` name successfully without issues. That means the creation went fine. Now let's see how to update the records that are already created.

The `Set-DnsServerResourceRecord` cmdlet is used for modifying any DNS record. It takes two objects as input. One is an old DNS object that has original data and the other is a new DNS object that has the modified data. The code, with its description, is as follows:

```
#create object of existing DNS record
$OldDNSObj = Get-DnsServerResourceRecord -Name testpc20 -
    ComputerName TIBDC2 -RRType A -ZoneName techibee.ad
#make a clone of old object and name it as new
$newDNSObj = $OldDNSObj.Clone()
#Update the IP Address in object
$newDNSObj.Recorddata.IPv4Address = "10.10.101.40"
#set the modified information on the A record
Set-DnsServerResourceRecord -NewInputObject $newDNSObj -
    OldInputObject $OldDNSObj -ComputerName TIBDC2 -ZoneName
    techibee.ad -PassThru
```

As you see in the preceding code, we first query the A type record using the `Get-DnsServerResourceRecord` cmdlet and stored in the `$OldDNSObj` variable and then made a clone of it, which is stored in the `$newDNSObj` variable. Then we modify the IP address stored in the new object. Both these new and old objects are passed to the `Set-DnsServerResourceRecord` cmdlet to implement the change.

The results can be verified using the `Resolve-DnsName` cmdlet, as shown in the following command:

```
PS C:\> Resolve-DnsName -Name testpc20 -Server TIBDC2  | fl


Name       : testpc20.techibee.ad
Type       : A
TTL        : 3600
DataLength : 4
Section    : Answer
IPAddress  : 10.10.101.40


PS C:\>
```

The result shows that the new IP address came into effect.

Now let's look at the procedure for deleting A type resource record. The `Remove-DnsServerResourceRecord` cmdlet does this task for us, as shown in the following command:

```
Remove-DnsServerResourceRecord -ZoneName techibee.ad -ComputerName
   TIBDC2 -RRType A -Name testpc20 -Force
```

Deletion is simple and straightforward. You need to specify the name of the record, type, zone name, and the DNS server name. The record will get deleted and replicated to other DCs as part of the AD replication schedule.

Managing CNAME records

The previous section discussed how to create, modify, and delete A type resource record. The same applies to the CNAME records as well with slight adjustments in parameters. So without much explanation, let's look at the code required for managing CNAME records.

The CNAME record can be created using the following command. It creates a CNAME (DC2) pointing to `TIBDC2.techibee.ad` A record:

```
Add-DnsServerResourceRecord -ZoneName techibee.ad -ComputerName
   TIBDC2 -Name DC2 -CName  -HostNameAlias tibdc2.techibee.ad
```

The `Resolve-DnsName` cmdlet shows these mapping details, as shown in the following command:

```
PS C:\> Resolve-DnsName -Name dc2 -Server TIBDC2


Name                     Type   TTL   Section   NameHost
----                     ----   ---   -------   --------
dc2.techibee.ad          CNAME  3600  Answer    tibdc2.techibee.ad


Name       : tibdc2.techibee.ad
QueryType  : A
TTL        : 3600
Section    : Answer
IP4Address : 10.10.101.10


PS C:\>
```

To modify the CNAME record, the following code can be used:

```
#create object of existing DNS record
$OldDNSObj = Get-DnsServerResourceRecord -Name DC2 -ComputerName
TIBDC2 -RRType Cname -ZoneName techibee.ad
#make a clone of old object and name it as new
$newDNSObj = $OldDNSObj.Clone()
#Update the IP Address in object
$newDNSObj.Recorddata.HostNameAlias = "tibdc3.techibee.ad"
#set the modified information on the A record
Set-DnsServerResourceRecord -NewInputObject $newDNSObj -OldInputObject
$OldDNSObj -ComputerName TIBDC2 -ZoneName techibee.ad -PassThru
```

Use the `Resolve-DnsName` cmdlet to verify the change, as shown in the following command:

```
PS C:\> Resolve-DnsName -Name dc2 -Server TIBDC2
```

Name	Type	TTL	Section	NameHost
dc2.techibee.ad	CNAME	3600	Answer	tibdc3.techibee.ad

```
PS C:\>
```

To delete the CNAME record, we can use the same cmdlet that we used for deleting A records, as shown in the following command:

```
Remove-DnsServerResourceRecord  -ZoneName techibee.ad -ComputerName
  TIBDC2 -RRType CName -Name DC2 -Force
```

The other records (MX, NS, PTR, and SOA) can be managed in a similar way using the same set of cmdlets.

Managing DNS Clients

So far we have seen different DNS sever-related operations in this chapter. As mentioned at the beginning of this chapter, a module is available for managing the client-side operations related to DNS. It can be loaded using the following command:

```
Import-Module DnsClient
```

In the previous section, we used the `Resolve-Dnsname` cmdlet from this module, which helps in resolving the DNS names. The following are some of the frequent DNS operations that are performed from the client's-side and sample codes:

Get client-side DNS cache. This is equivalent to the `ipconfig /displaydns` command in Windows as shown in the following command:

```
Get-DnsClientCache
```

The client-side cache can be cleared by using the following command. This is equivalent to the `ipconfig /flushdns` command:

```
Clear-DnsClientCache
```

The following command displays the DNS servers configured on the `LabNet` network interface:

```
Get-DnsClientServerAddress -InterfaceAlias Labnet -AddressFamily Ipv4
```

DNS server IP addresses on the client-side can be changed using the following command:

```
Set-DnsClientServerAddress -InterfaceAlias Labnet -ServerAddresses
  @("10.10.101.25","10.10.101.10")
```

The `Set-DnsClientServerAddress` cmdlet has a switch parameter `-Validate` that verifies that the given DNS servers are valid and reachable before assigning them to a network interface. This validation is not performed when this parameter is not mentioned.

The existing list of DNS servers can be removed using the following command:

```
Set-DnsClientServerAddress -InterfaceAlias Labnet -
  ResetServerAddresses
```

This completes our quick stunt with DNS Client module. However, it is recommended to explore this module further, as it can perform other operations, that can help with your automated jobs.

Summary

In this chapter, we have learned how to automate DNS server-related operations and how to perform some client-side tasks using PowerShell modules. The DNSServer module has more than 100 cmdlets, and is each designed to perform a specific task. Though not all of these cmdlets are not covered here, it is advisable to go through them and understand their functionality. This will help in identifying the areas that you can automate using this PowerShell module.

The next chapter provides some resources useful for learning how to manage Active Directory using PowerShell and some PowerShell resources for improving your coding abilities. It also provides some sample scripts that you may want to use in your environment (of course after proper testing in the lab).

9
Miscellaneous Scripts and Resources for Further Learning

In previous chapters, you learned about using PowerShell and Active Directory modules to manage different AD objects. You also learned about managing the Active Directory configuration using PowerShell; I hope they gave you a good foundation to start your automation tasks. This chapter provides you with some useful and handy scripts to perform a designated task in Active Directory. There are several tasks that demand automation in Active Directory and it is difficult to cover all of them. So, this chapter gives you code samples to perform the following Active Directory operations, which are frequently used and common in most environments. These scripts come in handy for Windows administrators in their day-to-day operations.

The following is the list of scripts that we are going to discuss in this chapter. You will also find some useful resources and links at the end of this chapter for further learning and to get your questions answered, if any, about the following topics:

- Checking whether user, group, computer, and Organizational Unit exists
- Getting membership of a user, computer, and group
- Resetting the password for multiple user accounts
- Bulk creation of user accounts
- Getting the password expiry date of user accounts
- Finding all disabled user accounts
- Getting all domain controllers and their site names in the forest
- Moving objects from one OU to another

- Finding inactive computers in Active Directory
- Creating groups in bulk
- Exporting AD group member details to Comma Separated Value
- Finding empty groups in Active Directory
- Checking whether a user is a member of the given group or not
- Comparing AD group memberships

The code for the preceding topic is written in the form of functions rather than scripts. It is easy to reuse these functions and incorporate them into any of your existing scripts. These functions assume that you have already imported the Active Directory module. Most of these functions return the output in an object format so that they can be passed as input to any other function or cmdlet. You can also export such object-based outputs to a CSV file easily using the Export-CSV cmdlet.

Checking whether a user, group, computer, or an OU exists

Here is a simple script to check whether a user, computer, group, or OU exists in Active Directory with a given name. This script is capable of accepting multiple names and testing to see whether they exist:

```
Function Test-ADObject {
[CmdletBinding()]
Param(
  [Parameter(Mandatory=$true,Position=0)]
  [string[]]$Name,
  [Parameter(Mandatory=$true,Position=1)]
  [ValidateSet("User","Group","Computer","organizationalUnit")]
  [string]$Type
)
foreach($ObjName in $Name) {
  $OutputObj = New-Object -TypeName PSObject -Property @{
      Name = $ObjName;
      IsFound = $null;
      ObjectClass = $Type }
  try {
    $ObjOut = @(Get-ADObject -Filter { Name -eq $ObjName -and
    ObjectClass -eq $Type } -EA Stop)
```

```
    if($ObjOut.count -eq 0) {
      $OutputObj.IsFound = $false
    }

    if($ObjOut.Count -gt 1) {
      $OutputObj.IsFound = $false
      Write-Verbose "Multiple objects found with the name
      $ObjName"
    }

    if($ObjOut.Count -eq 1) {
      $OutputObj.IsFound = $true
    }
  } catch {
    $OutputObj.IsFound = $false
  }
  $OutputObj | select Name, ObjectClass, IsFound
}
}
```

Usage

- To check whether a user account exists, use the following command:

  `Test-ADObject -Name DaveW -Type User`

- To check whether a computer account exists, use the following command:

  `Test-ADObject -Name TIBDC2 -Type Computer`

- To pass the input names from a text file, `c:\temp\users.txt` to the
  command prompt, use the following command:

  `Test-ADObject -Name (Get-Content c:\temp\users.txt) -Type User`

- To export the test results into an Excel file, use the following command:

  `Test-ADObject -Name (Get-Content c:\temp\users.txt) -Type User`
  `  | Export-CSV c:\temp\User-Output.csv -NotypeInformation`

Getting membership of a user, computer, and group

The function used in this section will help in finding out the group membership of users, computers, or groups. The output of this function is the same as what you will see in the **MemberOf** tab in the object properties. This function takes two types of input. The first one is the Name parameter and it takes a list of objects for which you want to query the membership details. The second one is the Type parameter, which indicates the class of the objects that you supplied to the Name parameter:

```
Function Get-ADobjectMembership {
[CmdletBinding()]
param(
   [Parameter(Mandatory=$true,Position=0)]
   [string[]]$Name,
   [Parameter(Mandatory=$true,Position=1)]
   [ValidateSet("User","Group","Computer")]
   [string]$Type
)
Foreach($ObjName in $Name) {
    try {
        $MemberOf = @(Get-ADObject -Filter { Name -eq $ObjName
-and ObjectClass -eq $Type} -Properties MemberOf -EA Stop | select
-ExpandProperty MemberOf)
        if(!$MemberOf) {
            Write-Warning "$ObjName is not member of any Groups"
            Continue
        }
        foreach($Group in $MemberOf) {
            $OutputObj = New-Object -TypeName PSObject -Property
            @{
                    Name = $ObjName;
                    MemberOf = $null
                }
            $GroupName = (Get-ADGroup -Identity $Group -EA
            Stop).Name
            $OutputObj.MemberOf = $GroupName
            $OutputObj
        }
    } catch {
        Write-Warning "Failed to query Membership of $ObjName. $_"
        Continue
    }
}
}
```

Usage

After copying the preceding code to PowerShell Window, you can use it to query the membership details of an AD object, as follows:

- To query the groups that a user belongs to, use the following command:

  ```
  PS C:\> Get-ADobjectMembership -Name LabUser100 -Type User
  ```

- To query the groups that a computer belongs to, use the following command:

  ```
  PS C:\> Get-ADobjectMembership -Name COMP1 -Type Computer
  ```

- To query the groups that a group belongs to, use the following command:

  ```
  PS C:\> Get-ADobjectMembership -Name ChildGroup1 -Type Group
  ```

You can pass multiple names to the Name parameter either as comma-separated values or by reading from a text file.

Resetting the password for multiple user accounts

Often, Windows administrators get requests to reset the password for a bunch of users. You can do this via a GUI approach if you have the time and patience. Otherwise, use the following function, which is an efficient way to do this. This function prompts for the password that you want to set for the users. This password should match the password complexity policy of your domain. You can pass the list of users to the UserName parameter either as a Comma-Separated Value or by reading from a text file:

```
Function Reset-ADuserPassword {
[CmdletBinding()]
Param(
    [string[]]$UserName
)
$Password = Read-Host "Enter the password that you want to set for the
users" -AsSecureString
foreach($User in $UserName) {
    try {
        Set-ADAccountPassword -Identity $User -Reset -NewPassword
        $Password -EA Stop
        Write-Host "Password successfully changed for $user"
    } catch {
        Write-Warning "Failed to reset password for $user. $_"
    }
}
}
```

Usage

Copy the preceding code into PowerShell Window and reset a user account password with the following command:

```
PS C:\> Reset-ADuserPassword -UserName spamarth
```

You can reset password for multiple user accounts by passing the list of usernames to the `-UserName` parameter.

Bulk creation of user accounts

In *Chapter 2, Managing User and Computer Objects*, we discussed the procedure to create user accounts in bulk. The code discussed here gives you a high-level overview of what is needed to read details from a CSV file and create user accounts using those details. The script in the following code is a much enhanced version and gives all the required code to create user accounts in bulk. One thing to note here is, as part of the account creation process, we are only setting up a few properties. But the real-time requirements might be different. So, you can use the code here as a sample reference and add more properties as you need so that you can adopt it in your environment. The input `BulkUserCreation.csv` file, which is used by this script, is also available along with the code samples. You can download it along with the script and make modifications accordingly.

Another thing to note here is that this script sets a default password for all the accounts created and keeps them in a disabled state. You can have a separate script to reset the password for users and enable them:

```powershell
#Save this code into a file and name as PS1
#Ex : Invoke-ADBulkUserCreation.ps1
[CmdletBinding()]
Param(
  [Parameter(Mandatory=$true,Position=0)]
  [ValidateScript({Test-Path $_})]
  [string[]]$CSVFilePath
)
try {
  $CSVData = @(Import-CSV -Path $CSVFilePath -EA Stop)
    Write-Host "Successfully imported entries from $CSVFilePath"
    Write-Host "Total no. of entries in CSV are :
    $($CSVData.count)"
} catch {
    Write-Host "Failed to read from the CSV file $CSVFilePath.
    Script exiting"
```

```
        return
}


foreach($Entry in $CSVData) {
#Verify that mandatory properties are defined for each object
$Name = $Entry.Name
$SamAccountName = $Entry.SAMAccountName
$GivenName = $Entry.GivenName
$SurName = $Entry.LastName
$Email = $Entry.Email
$StreetAddress = $Entry.Address
$City = $Entry.City
$Country = $Entry.Country
$State = $Entry.State
$Company = $Entry.Company
$EmployeeID = $Entry.EmployeeID
$Path = $Entry.OUName
$Password = "Randompwd1$"


if(!$Name) {
    Write-Warning "$Name is not provided. Continue to the next
    record"
    Continue
}
if(!$SamAccountName) {
    Write-Warning "$SamAccountName is not provided. Continue to
    the next record"
    Continue
}
if($Country.Length -ne 2) {
    Write-Warning "Country code should be of 2 characters only.
    Setting it to US for now"
    $Country = "US"
}
try {
    New-ADUser -Name $Name `
                -SamAccountName $SamAccountName `
                -GivenName $GivenName `
                -Surname $SurName `
                -EmailAddress $Email `
                -AccountPassword (ConvertTo-SecureString -String
                $Password -AsPlainText -Force) `
                -StreetAddress $StreetAddress `
                -City $City `
```

```
                -State $State `
                -Country $Country `
                -Company $Company `
                -EmployeeID $EmployeeID `
                -Enabled $false `
                -Path $Path
    Write-host "$Name : User Account created successfully"
} catch {
    Write-Warning "$Name : Error occurred while creating account.
    $_"
}
}
```

Usage

Save the preceding code into a file called `Invoke-ADBulkUserCreation.ps1` and prepare the input CSV with the required user creation details. The input CSV template is available along with the code samples that you got with this book. Once the file is ready, you can execute the script to read details from the CSV and create user accounts, as shown in the following command:

```
PS C:\scripts> .\Invoke-ADBulkUserCreation.ps1 -CSVFilePath
  C:\scripts\BulkUserCreation.csv
```

The preceding command reads details from the `C:\scripts\BulkUserCreation.csv` file and creates the user accounts. The output will show whether the creation is successful or not.

Getting the password expiry date of user accounts

The function discussed in this section helps in retrieving the password expiry date of the users in the domain. The good thing with this function is that it makes use of the `msDS-UserPasswordExpiryTimeComputed` attribute of the user accounts to determine the password expiry date. This attribute stores a dynamic value that indicates the date and time when the password of the user is going to expire. This value will be in the `FileTime` format. This function looks for user accounts that are enabled and has the `PasswordNeverExpires` attribute set to `false`:

```
Function Get-PasswordExpiryDetails {
[CmdletBinding()]
Param(
)
```

```
$Users = Get-ADUser -Filter {PasswordNeverExpires -eq $false -and
   Enabled -eq $true} `-Properties msDS-
   UserPasswordExpiryTimeComputed,*

Foreach($User in $Users) {
   $OutputObj = New-Object -TypeName PSObject -Property @{
         UserName = $User.Name;
         DisplayName = $null;
         PwdExpirtyDate = $null;
         PwdExpiryInDays = $Null
      }
   $ExpiryDate = [DateTime]::FromFileTime($User."msDS-
   UserPasswordExpiryTimeComputed")
   $ExpirtyInDays = ($ExpiryDate - (Get-Date)).Days
   $OutputObj.DisplayName = $User.DisplayName
   $OutputObj.PwdExpirtyDate = $ExpiryDate
   $OutputObj.PwdExpiryInDays = $ExpirtyInDays
   $OutputObj
   }
}
```

Usage

Import the preceding function into any of the PowerShell Windows where you have an Active Directory module and get the password expiry details of all the users in the current domain using following command:

```
PS C:\> Get-PasswordExpiryDetails
```

The output of the preceding command displays the **Name**, **DisplayName**, **Expiry in days**, and **Date of Expiry** fields of the user accounts.

If you want to sort the results so the accounts that are going to expire first appear at the top, then use the following command:

```
PS C:\> Get-PasswordExpiryDetails | Sort PwdExpiryIndays
```

UserName	PwdExpiryInDays	DisplayName	PwdExpirtyDate
ChrisB	-23	Chris Brown	19/10/2014 7:56:36 AM
JohnM	-23	John Miller	19/10/2014 7:56:36 AM
Johnw	-23	John Williams	19/10/2014 7:18:07 AM
Labuser100	39		21/12/2014 12:50:53 AM
DaveW	39	Dave Williams	21/12/2014 1:20:32 AM

```
PS C:\>
```

As you can see in the preceding command, the accounts that are already expired are shown at the top. Export the results into a CSV file, if you are more comfortable with Excel and want to do further filtering there.

The results can be exported by piping the output to the Export-CSV cmdlet.

Finding all the disabled user accounts

Finding disabled user accounts in Active Directory is very simple. Each user object returned by the Get-ADuser cmdlet will have an Enabled property, which holds the value False when the user account is in the disabled state. Examining this value for all the user accounts in the domain will tell us how many accounts are currently in the disabled state.

The following script will query the current domain for disabled users and the exports to the CSV filename disabled-users.csv in the C:\temp folder. Make sure that the c:\temp folder exists, or you change the $OutputFilePath variable's value in the code to a folder path where you want the output to be placed:

```
Function Find-DisabledUsers {
[CmdletBinding()]
param(
)
$OutputFilePath = "c:\temp\Disabled-Users.csv"
Add-Content -Path $OutputFilePath -Value "UserName, DisplayName,
  DistinguishedName"
$DisabledUsers = Get-ADUser -Filter { Enabled -eq $false } -
  Properties DisplayName
foreach($User in $disabledUsers) {
Add-Content -Path $OutputFilePath -Value ("{0},{1},'{2}'" -f
  $User.Name, $User.DisplayName, $User.DistinguishedName)
}
}
```

Output

The preceding code helps you in identifying the disabled accounts in the domain. It searches Active Directory for disabled accounts and writes the details to the c:\temp\Disabled-Users.csv file. This function doesn't require any arguments. Executing the command shown in the following code will generate the output:

```
PS C:\> Find-DisabledUsers
```

If the output file already exists, it appends the data to it.

Getting all domain controllers and their site names in the forest

The function discussed in this section is a simple wrapper on top of the
Get-ADDomainController cmdlet to query all the domain controllers in forest
and display frequently referred-to details, such as DC name, domain name, site
name — whether these names are global catalog servers or not — and reachability
of the domain controller:

```
Function Get-DCDetails {
[CmdletBinding()]
Param(
)
$Domains = (Get-ADForest).Domains
$DCs = $Domains | % { Get-ADDomainController -Filter * -Server $_
    }
foreach($DC in $DCs) {
  $OutputObj = New-Object -TypeName PSObject -Property @{
          DCName = $User.Name;
          DCDomain = $null;
          IsGC = $null;
          SiteName = $Null;
          IsOnline = $null
      }
  if(Test-Connection -Computer $DC -Count 1 -quiet) {
    $OutputObj.IsOnline = $true
  } else {
    $OutputObj.IsOnline = $false
  }
    $OutputObj.DCName = $DC.HostName
  $OutputObj.DCDomain = $DC.Domain
  $OutputObj.IsGC = $DC.IsGlobalCatalog
  $OutputObj.SiteName = $DC.Site
  $OutputObj
}
}
```

Usage

The preceding code will display DC details in the forest. You just need to copy the
code into a PowerShell Window and call it with a function name, as shown in the
following command:

```
PS C:\> Get-DCDetails
```

One thing to remember here is that since the `Get-ADDomainController` cmdlet requires permissions to connect to all the DCs, you need to run this cmdlet as an Enterprise administrator; otherwise, the command execution will fail.

Moving objects from one OU to another

Often, Active Directory objects are moved between different OUs for reorganization purposes. The following script searches the AD for the given objects and moves them to the mentioned OU target. This script works for user, computer, and group object types:

```
Function Move-ObjectsToOU {
[CmdletBinding()]
param(
   [Parameter(Mandatory=$true,Position=0)]
   [string[]]$Name,
   [Parameter(Mandatory=$true,Position=1)]
   [ValidateSet("User","Group","Computer")]
   [string]$Type,
   [Parameter(Mandatory=$true,Position=2)]
   [string]$TargetOUPath
)
if([ADSI]::Exists("LDAP://{0}" -f $TargetOUPath)) {
  Foreach($ObjectName in $Name) {
    try {
      $Object = Get-ADObject -Filter { Name -eq $ObjectName -and
      ObjectClass -eq $Type } -EA Stop
      Move-ADObject -Identity $Object -TargetPath $TargetOUPath -
      EA Stop
      Write-Host "$ObjectName : Moved successfully to target OU"
    } catch {
      Write-Warning "Cannot move $ObjectName"}
    }
} else {
  Write-Warning "The target OU not found. Script exiting"
}
}
```

Usage

- To move users in a text file to LAB OU, use the following command:

```
Move-ObjectsToOU -Name (get-content c:\temp\users.txt) -Type
    User -TargetOUPath "OU=Prod,DC=techibee,DC=ad"
```

- To move computers in a text file to LAB OU, use the following command:

```
Move-ObjectsToOU -Name (get-content c:\temp\comps.txt) -Type
    Computer -TargetOUPath "OU=Prod,DC=techibee,DC=ad"
```

Finding inactive computers in Active Directory

A computer's inactivity is decided based on when that computer account had its password changed last time. A computer account changes its password in Active Directory every 30 days by default. So, any computer that had its password last set longer than 30 days ago, it will mean that the computer is not connected to the network for some reason. It could be either decommissioned, crashed, or made offline for troubleshooting. The following function will help you query computers older than the given number of days:

```
Function Find-InactiveComputers {
[CmdletBinding()]
Param(
   [int]$DaysOlderThan
)
$older = (Get-Date).AddDays(-$DaysOlderThan)
Get-ADComputer -Filter { PasswordLastSet -lt $older } | select
   Name, DistinguishedName
}
```

Usage

Query computers that are inactive for more than 40 days using following command:

```
Find-InactiveComputers -DaysOlderThan 40
```

This displays the name and distinguished name of the computer accounts that are older than 40 days.

Creating groups in bulk

Previously, we have seen bulk creation of users using PowerShell. A similar requirement might come from creating security groups in bulk. The function given in the following code helps in creating groups in a bulk fashion. It creates a security group of a given scope (domain local, global, or universal) inside the default user's container by default. They can be created in different locations in the Active Directory structure by updating the `$TargetOU` variable's value with the DN of the OU where you want to create them:

```
Function Invoke-ADBulkGroup {
[CmdletBinding()]
Param(
  [Parameter(Mandatory=$true, Position = 0)]
  [String[]]$GroupName,
  [Parameter(Mandatory=$true, Position = 1)]
  [ValidateSet("DomainLocal","Global","Universal")]
  [string]$GroupScope
)
#Change the value of $TargetOU variable to the DN of the path
  where you want the groups to be created
#If you leave it, it will create in default users container.
$TargetOU = (Get-ADDomain).UsersContainer
#$TargetOU = "OU=Prod1,DC=techibee,DC=ad"

if(!([ADSI]::Exists("LDAP://$TargetOU"))) {
  Write-Warning "The given OU $TargetOU not found. Exiting"
  return
}

Foreach($Group in $GroupName) {
try {
  $GroupObj = Get-ADGroup -Identity $Group -EA Stop
  if($GroupObj) {
    Write-Warning "$Group : Group already exists. Cannot create
    another with same name"
    Continue
  }
} catch {
  try {
    New-ADGroup -Name $Group -GroupScope $GroupScope -EA Stop
    Write-Host "$Group : Successfully Created"
  } catch {
    Write-Warning "$Group : An error occurred during creation"
  }
}
}
}
```

Usage

To create multiple groups in one go, you can use the following command after importing the preceding function into a PowerShell Window:

```
PS C:\> Invoke-ADBulkGroup -GroupName Sales-INDIA,Sales-US,Sales-
   Singapore -GroupScope Global
```

Groups can be created by reading the names from the text file. Use the following command that reads group names from the `c:\temp\groups.txt` file and creates domainlocal security groups with these names:

```
PS C:\> Invoke-ADBulkGroup -GroupName (Get-Content
   c:\temp\groups.txt) -GroupScope DomainLocal
```

This function first checks whether the group exists in Active Directory and then proceeds with creating it.

Exporting an AD group member's details to CSV

Often, end users enquire about the membership of a particular group or list of groups. It is the job of Windows administrators to help them with the information in a format that is most suitable for them. We generally share such information in Excel (or CSV format). But this CSV preparation is not an easy task if there are nested members, and the number of groups you want to generate this report for are more. The function discussed in the following code can help here. It takes a list of group names as input and exports the membership details to a CSV file. At the time of export, we can choose whether to export direct members only or nested members as well:

```
Function Export-ADGroupMembers {
[CmdletBinding()]
Param(
   [Parameter(Mandatory=$true)]
   [String[]]$GroupName,
   [Switch]$Nested
)
$MemArray = @()
foreach($Group in $GroupName) {
   try {
      $GroupMem = @(Get-ADGroupMember -Identity $Group -
      Recursive:$Nested -EA Stop)
      if(!$GroupMem) {
```

```
        Write-Warning "$Group has no members"
        Continue
    }
    foreach($Mem in $GroupMem) {
        $Mem = $Mem |select name, SamAccountName, objectClass
        $Mem | Add-Member -MemberType NoteProperty -Name GroupName -
        Value $Group
        $MemArray += $Mem
    }
} catch {
    Write-Warning "Error occurred while querying $Group"
    }
    }
}

$MemArray | select GroupName, name, SamAccountName, objectClass
    | Export-CSV c:\temp\GroupMembeship.csv -NotypeInformation
Write-Host "Output available at c:\temp\GroupMembeship.Csv"
    }
```

Usage

The usage of this function is simple. After copying the preceding code to PowerShell Window, just call name by passing its name of the group that you want to export the membership to the group, as shown in the following command:

```
PS C:\> Export-ADGroupMembers -GroupName ChildGroup100
```

By default, it will export the direct members, and the exported file is available in the c:\temp folder with the GroupMembeship.csv name. You can change this path in the code if you want.

You can also export the nested membership of a group using the -Nested switch:

```
PS C:\> Export-ADGroupMembers -GroupName ChildGroup100 -Nested
```

Multiple group names can be specified either by a comma separating them or by reading from a text file:

```
PS C:\> Export-ADGroupMembers -GroupName ChildGroup100,ChildGroup10 -
    Nested
```

The output that is exported to the CSV contains details about the group name, its member name, object class, and SamAccount name.

Finding empty groups in Active Directory

The PowerShell function discussed in this section helps you to find out the groups that have no members in them. This function has an optional switch parameter called -Nested, which indicates that a group has to be queried recursively for membership to determine whether it is empty or not. In some cases, a group can have another group in it, which might be empty as well. This switch will come in handy to find such cases:

```
Function Find-EmptyADGroups {
[CmdletBinding()]
Param(
   [switch]$Nested
)

$Groups = Get-ADGroup -Filter *
Write-Host "`nBelow is the list of empty groups in Active
   Directory`n`n"
$Count = 0
foreach($Group in $Groups) {
   $Members = Get-ADGroupMember -Identity $Group -Recursive:$Nested
   if(!$Members) {
      $Group | select Name, DistinguishedName
      $Count++
   }
}
Write-Host "`n`n`nTotal no. of empty groups are : $Count`n`n`n"
}
```

Usage

The usage of this code is very simple. Just copy and paste the preceding code into PowerShell Window where you have the Active Directory module imported, then run the following command to check the groups that are empty even at the -Nested level:

```
PS C:\> Find-EmptyADGroups -Nested
```

To find groups that don't have any direct members (includes groups) in them, use the following command:

```
PS C:\> Find-EmptyADGroups
```

The output of both the preceding commands shows the name and distinguished name of the groups that are empty. It also displays the number of empty groups it found at the end of the output.

Verifying whether a user is a member of the given group or not

Sometimes, there comes a need to check whether a user account is member of the particular AD group or not. If the group has no further groups in it, it is easy to verify it from either the user account's **Memberof** or **Groups Members** tab in ADUC. If the group has nested groups, it is difficult to go through each group and figure out whether the user account is member or not. The difficulty increases when you have multiple accounts to verify. The PowerShell function given in this section will simplify this task. It takes a single or list of usernames and checks whether they are members (including nested) of the given AD group. The output indicates the username, group name, and whether a user is a member or not:

```
Function Test-IsGroupMember {
[CmdletBinding()]
param(
    [Parameter(Mandatory=$true,Position=0)]
    [string[]]$UserName,
    [Parameter(Mandatory=$true,Position=1)]
    [string]$GroupName
)

$GroupMembers = Get-ADGroupMember -Identity $GroupName -Recursive
    | ? {$_.objectClass -eq "User" }
if(!$GroupMembers) {
    Write-Warning "$GroupName : Group doesn't have any User
    accounts as members"
}

foreach($User in $UserName) {
$OutputObj = New-Object -TypeName PSObject -Property @{
        UserName = $User;
        GroupName = $GroupName;
        IsMember = $False
    }
foreach($Member in $GroupMembers) {
    if($User -eq $Member.Name) {
        $OutputObj.IsMember = $True
    }
}
}
$OutputObj
}
}
```

Usage

You can copy and paste the preceding code into the PowerShell Window and start using it. To check whether a user account is part of a group called `ChildGroup100`, use the following command:

```
PS C:\> Test-IsGroupMember -UserName labuser100 -GroupName
   ChildGroup100
```

If you want to verify this for two or three users, use the command shown here:

```
PS C:\> Test-IsGroupMember -UserName labuser100,labuser120 -GroupName
   ChildGroup100
```

You can also provide user's list from a text file using the following command:

```
PS C:\> Test-IsGroupMember -UserName (Get-Content c:\temp\users.txt)
   -GroupName ChildGroup100
```

The output is in object format, so you can easily export it to CSV using the `Export-CSV` cmdlet.

Comparing AD groups' membership

Sometimes, you might find a need to compare membership of two security groups. This is generally required to find whether they are identical. This not only helps in getting rid of duplicate groups, but also in troubleshooting permission issues. The function discussed in the following code takes two group names as input and compares their members. The output contains a report that shows the number of objects that exist in both the groups, and the number of objects that are found in the first group but not the second and vice versa:

```
Function Compare-ADGroups {
[CmdletBinding()]
Param(
   [Parameter(Mandatory=$true, Position = 0)]
   [String]$Group1,
   [Parameter(Mandatory=$true, Position = 1)]
   [String]$Group2,
   [Parameter(Position = 2)]
   [switch]$Nested
)
try {
   $Group1Obj = @(Get-ADGroupMember -Identity $Group1 -
   Recursive:$Nested -EA Stop)
```

```
    $Group2Obj = @(Get-ADGroupMember -Identity $Group2 -
    Recursive:$Nested -EA Stop)
  } catch {
    Write-Warning "Failed to query group members."
    return
  }
  if(!$Group1Obj) {
    Write-Warning "$Group1 is empty. Nothing to Compare"
    Continue
  }
  if(!$Group2Obj) {
    Write-Warning "$Group2 is empty. Nothing to Compare"
    Continue
  }
  $DiffObj = Compare-Object -ReferenceObject $Group1Obj `-
  DifferenceObject $Group2Obj `-IncludeEqual
  $CommonObj = @()
  $FoundIn1 = @()
  $FoundIn2 = @()

  foreach($Obj in $DiffObj) {
    if($Obj.SideIndicator -eq "==") {
      $CommonObj +=$Obj
    }
    if($Obj.SideIndicator -eq "=>") {
      $FoundIn2 +=$Obj
    }
    if($Obj.SideIndicator -eq "<=") {
      $FoundIn1 +=$Obj
    }
  }

  Write-host "Members found in both the Groups :
  $($CommonObj.count)"
  Write-host ""
  $CommonObj.InputObject | select Name,ObjectClass
  Write-host ""
  Write-host "Members found in $Group1 but not in $Group2  :
  $($FoundIn1.count)"
  Write-host ""
  $FoundIn1.InputObject | select Name,ObjectClass
  Write-host ""
  Write-host "Members found in $Group2 but not in $Group1  :
  $($FoundIn2.count)"
  Write-host ""
  $FoundIn2.InputObject | select Name,ObjectClass
  Write-host ""
}
```

Usage

Using the preceding function is simple. After copying the preceding code into a PowerShell Window where you have an Active Directory module imported, execute the following command to compare the membership of two groups. Here, we are comparing `ChildGroup1` and `TestGroup1`:

```
PS C:\> Compare-ADGroups -Group1 ChildGroup1 -Group2 TestGroup1
```

As mentioned earlier, the preceding command compares the objects that are added directly. If you would like to compare nested members as well, then use the `-Nested` switch:

```
PS C:\> Compare-ADGroups -Group1 ChildGroup1 -Group2 TestGroup1 -
   Nested
```

In both the preceding cases, the output will contain the `Name` and `Object` class of the members that are found in both the groups and extra ones.

Resources for further learning

Learning is the key to become expert in any topic, and it should be a continuous exercise. There are several resources freely available on the Internet to learn about PowerShell and managing Active Directory using it. In this section, let's look at some of these resources using which you can further increase your knowledge.

PowerShell resources

There are several good books available from Packt Publising that are based on PowerShell. These books will help you to understand how to use the cmdlets available in the Active Directory module from PowerShell's perspective. You should definitely take a look at these books to get yourself familiarized with PowerShell. You can find a few of them towards the end of the book.

Looking for some books to learn PowerShell? The community of PowerShell is super awesome. Many experts have written books to help the PowerShell community and made them available free of cost. A collection of free books is available at `http://powershell.org/wp/ebooks`.

`PowerShell.org` makes every attempt to make this page up to date with the new free books that are being announced to the community.

Some other resources that can provide you with free material are as follows:

- Visit TechNet-blog at `http://blogs.technet.com/b/pstips/archive/2014/05/26/free-powershell-ebooks.aspx`.

- Visit Techibee.com at `http://techibee.com/powershell/powershell-collection-of-free-e-books-for-download/1503`.

- The Windows PowerShell Survival guide at `http://social.technet.microsoft.com/wiki/contents/articles/183.windows-powershell-survival-guide.aspx`. This has lots of resources useful to learn PowerShell.

- Visit Hey Scripting Guy's blog at `http://blogs.technet.com/b/heyscriptingguy/`.

Active Directory resources

To learn more about managing Active Directory using PowerShell, the help content of cmdlets in the Active Directory module is the first source. An explanation about each cmdlet, their parameters, and examples gives more details about the cmdlet and their use cases.

To get help content of a cmdlet in the Active Directory module, use `Get-Help`:

```
Get-Help <cmdlet name> -Full
```

You can also get the same content from the TechNet website at `http://technet.microsoft.com/en-us/library/ee617195.aspx`.

The preceding link contains help content of all the cmdlets. If you want to view help for a given cmdlet, you can try the following command:

```
Get-Help <cmdlet name> -Online
```

Learning about these cmdlets is not everything. To manage Active Directory using PowerShell, you should have sound knowledge of it. There are many good books on Active Directory from Packt Publishing.

The TechNet gallery has good number of scripts to manage Active Directory. Following are some of the links that you may want to look at scripts for various purposes:

- User Account Management (`http://goo.gl/e2TiKM`)
- Computer Account Management (`http://goo.gl/K9ao3J`)
- Groups Management (`http://goo.gl/DJZTSt`)
- Working with OUs (`http://goo.gl/M1LcWh`)
- Searching Active Directory (`http://goo.gl/CSKAp1`)

You can get some more resources about managing Active Directory with Active Directory from `http://technet.microsoft.com/en-us/scriptcenter/dd793613.aspx`, which leads you to several other resources, logs, script galleries (including previous), and articles.

Also, there are some good blogs from individuals that give real-world examples and insights. One such blog from a Microsoft PFE is `http://blogs.technet.com/b/ashleymcglone/`.

If you would like to work with SID history during the accounts migration process, you can check out the SIDHistory module at `https://gallery.technet.microsoft.com/scriptcenter/PowerShell-Module-for-08769c67`.

Above all, use your favorite search engine to get the sample code for specific requirements. One suggestion is that you should always understand the code and test it in a lab environment before trying it out in production. Without proper understanding of the code and lack of testing, it can cause serious problems. This is not just with PowerShell and is the same for any programming language.

I hope you found this book helpful.

Index

New Technology File System (NTFS)
    permissions 42
NS records 177

O

objects
    moving, from one OU to another 196, 197
Organizational Units (OUs)
    creating 88, 89
    deleting 92
    existence, checking 186
    managing 84
    modifying 89-91
    moving 92
    renaming 91
    searching for 85-87

P

password
    resetting, for multiple user accounts 189
Password Settings Objects (PSO) 114
Policy Settings Container (PSC) 114
PowerShell
    resources 205, 206
    used, for managing Active Directory 7, 8
Primary Domain Controller (PDC)
    emulator 64
primary zone, DNS zones 173
PTR records
    about 177
    managing 178-180

Q

Quest
    about 13
    installing 13
Quest AD PowerShell cmdlets
    about 12
    functionality, testing 14
    Quest, installing 13
Quest AD module 12
Quest AD Snap-in 13

R

Read-Only Domain Controller (RODC) 82
recursion
    about 165
    disabling 165
    enabling 165
Remove-ADComputer cmdlet 38
Remove-ADGroup cmdlet 59
Remove-ADGroupMember cmdlet 56
Remove-ADOrganizationalUnit cmdlet 92
Remove-ADReplicationSite cmdlet 97
Remove-ADReplicationSubnet cmdlet 97
Remove-ADUser cmdlet 32
Remove-DfsnFolderTarget cmdlet 142
Remove-DfsReplicationGroup cmdlet 155
Remove-DnsServerForwarder cmdlet 170
Remove-DnsServerResourceRecord
    cmdlet 181
Remove-GPLink cmdlet 78
Remote Server Administration
    Tools. See RSAT
Remove-WindowsFeature cmdlet 128
Rename-ADObject cmdlet 91
replication status, Active Directory
    obtaining 107-114
Resolve-Dnsname cmdlet 182
Resolve-DnsName cmdlet 180, 181
resources
    Active Directory resources 206, 207
    PowerShell resources 205, 206
Restore-ADObject cmdlet 121, 124
Resultant Set Of Policies (RSOP) data
    collecting remotely 77
root hints
    about 166
    configuring 168
    configuring, in DNS 167-170
RSAT
    about 9, 61
    installing 10

S

Search-ADAccount cmdlet 36
secondary zone, DNS zones 173

Thank you for buying
Active Directory with PowerShell

About Packt Publishing

Packt, pronounced 'packed', published its first book, *Mastering phpMyAdmin for Effective MySQL Management*, in April 2004, and subsequently continued to specialize in publishing highly focused books on specific technologies and solutions.

Our books and publications share the experiences of your fellow IT professionals in adapting and customizing today's systems, applications, and frameworks. Our solution-based books give you the knowledge and power to customize the software and technologies you're using to get the job done. Packt books are more specific and less general than the IT books you have seen in the past. Our unique business model allows us to bring you more focused information, giving you more of what you need to know, and less of what you don't.

Packt is a modern yet unique publishing company that focuses on producing quality, cutting-edge books for communities of developers, administrators, and newbies alike. For more information, please visit our website at www.packtpub.com.

About Packt Enterprise

In 2010, Packt launched two new brands, Packt Enterprise and Packt Open Source, in order to continue its focus on specialization. This book is part of the Packt Enterprise brand, home to books published on enterprise software – software created by major vendors, including (but not limited to) IBM, Microsoft, and Oracle, often for use in other corporations. Its titles will offer information relevant to a range of users of this software, including administrators, developers, architects, and end users.

Writing for Packt

We welcome all inquiries from people who are interested in authoring. Book proposals should be sent to author@packtpub.com. If your book idea is still at an early stage and you would like to discuss it first before writing a formal book proposal, then please contact us; one of our commissioning editors will get in touch with you.

We're not just looking for published authors; if you have strong technical skills but no writing experience, our experienced editors can help you develop a writing career, or simply get some additional reward for your expertise.

Windows Server 2012 Automation with PowerShell Cookbook

ISBN: 978-1-84968-946-5   Paperback: 372 pages

Over 110 recipes to automate Windows Server administrative tasks using PowerShell

1. Extend the capabilities of your Windows environment.

2. Improve the process reliability by using well defined PowerShell scripts.

3. Full of examples, scripts, and real-world best practices.

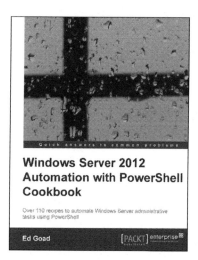

Instant Migration from Windows Server 2008 and 2008 R2 to 2012 How-to

ISBN: 978-1-84968-744-7   Paperback: 84 pages

A step-by-step guide to installing, configuring, and updating to Windows Server 2012

1. Learn something new in an Instant! A short, fast, focused guide delivering immediate results.

2. Install and configure Windows Server 2012 and upgrade Active Directory.

3. Decommission old servers and convert your environment into the Windows Server 2012 native environment.

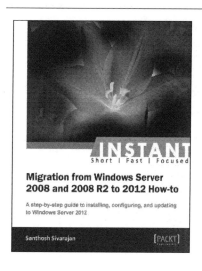

Please check **www.PacktPub.com** for information on our titles

Windows Server 2012 Hyper-V: Deploying Hyper-V Enterprise Server Virtualization Platform

ISBN: 978-1-84968-834-5   Paperback: 410 pages

Build Hyper-V infrastructure with secured multitenancy, flexible infrastructure, scalability, and high availability

1. A complete step-by-step Hyper-V deployment guide, covering all Hyper-V features for configuration and management best practices.

2. Understand multi-tenancy, flexible architecture, scalability, and high availability features of new Windows Server 2012 Hyper-V.

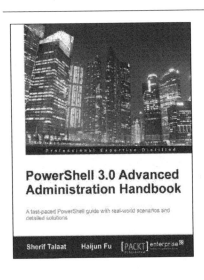

PowerShell 3.0 Advanced Administration Handbook

ISBN: 978-1-84968-642-6   Paperback: 370 pages

A fast-paced PowerShell guide with real-world scenarios and detailed solutions

1. Discover and understand the concept of Windows PowerShell 3.0.

2. Learn the advanced topics and techniques for a professional PowerShell scripting.

3. Explore the secret of building custom PowerShell snap-ins and modules.

Please check **www.PacktPub.com** for information on our titles